W9-BKJ-076

The Little Book
on
Oral Argument

Alan L. Dworsky

Fred B. Rothman Publications
Littleton, Colorado 80127
1991

Library of Congress Cataloging-in-Publication Data

Dworsky, Alan L.
  The little book on oral argument / Alan L. Dworsky.

     p. cm.
     ISBN 0-8377-0557-6

   1. Oral pleading—United States.   I. Title.
KF8870.D89   1991
347.73' 72—dc 20
[347.30772]   91-22872
                                             CIP

Thirteenth printing 2015

For copies of this book or other books
by Alan L. Dworsky, please call
William S. Hein & Co., Inc., at 800-828-7571

Printed in the United States of America

This volume is printed on acid-free paper.

Fred B. Rothman Publications

a division of
William S. Hein & Co., Inc.
Buffalo, New York

To my mom

Thanks to all who read and commented on the manuscript of this book: Professor Cathy Deal, Moot Court Advisor, Hamline University School of Law; Cynthia Lehr, Chief Attorney for the Minnesota Court of Appeals; Anne McKinsey, Hennepin County District Judge; Kathleen Mahoney, attorney at Oppenheimer, Wolff & Donnelly in St. Paul; Susan Andrews, appellate attorney in the Minnesota Public Defender's office; Paul G. Stoltz, Professor of Communication at Northern Arizona University and principal of PEAK Learning Consultants; my editors Shannon Wingrove and Paul Rothman; and my cousin Aaron Shure, street performer at Disney World.

But I owe more than thanks to my wife, Betsy Sansby, an editor mercilessly honest, tireless and thorough, playful and poetic, my partner and friend. Co-author on parts of this book, midwife to others, she showed respect for the words that were right and none for those that were wrong. Digging and planting, clipping and pruning, weeding and watering, she tended this garden of prose. There are many of her flowers in this book.

Contents

1 Introduction—1

2 Nervousness—3

3 Preparation—9

4 Style—24

5 Delivery—37

6 Substance—48

7 Structure—56

8 Questions—64

9 Rebuttal—72

10 Conclusion—77

Detailed Table of Contents

1   Introduction—1

2   Nervousness—3
Oral argument is scary—3
Nervousness is normal—3
Controlled nervousness can be useful—4
Nervousness usually disappears soon after you start
     arguing—4
Most nervousness doesn't show—4
Most judges want you to do well—4
Identify with your client's cause—5
Get in touch with your body—6
Breathe properly—6
Watch as many oral arguments as you can—7
Visualize success—7
Prepare thoroughly—7

3   Preparation—9
Know the record—9
Know the law—9
Know the court—10
Know the rules—11
Anticipate questions—12
Know your teammate's arguments—13
Make an outline—14
Plan what you will bring to the podium—16
Think twice before using a visual aid in an appellate
     court—18
Perfect your writing—21

Practice your argument—21
Check out the courtroom—22
Give yourself a break—23
Arrive at the courtroom early—23

4   Style—24
You can't be totally yourself—24
Speak in a conversational style—24
Use plain English—25
Avoid "I statements" in the body of your argument—26
Omit introductory phrases that weaken your
       arguments—27
Show respect for the court without fawning—27
Refer to the opposing party, not the opposing
       advocate—29
Call your teammate your "co-counsel"—30
Get serious—30
Show appropriate emotion—31
Convey that you believe in your client's cause—32
Don't break character—33
There's no backstage—33
Deal calmly with distractions—34
Don't get down in the dirt with your opponent—35

5   Delivery—37
Wear appropriate clothes—37
Wear a conservative hairstyle—38
Stand straight—38
Rest your hands on the podium—39
Reinforce your words with gestures—40
Reinforce your words with facial expressions—40
Maintain eye contact with the judges—41
Don't read your argument—41
Don't memorize your argument—41
Speak up—42
Speak at a controlled speed—42

Speak at a pitch in the lower end of your range—43
Use vocal dynamics—43
Take out the "uhs"—43
Pronounce words correctly—44
Don't magnify your mistakes—47
Adjust your intensity to the distance between you and
    the judges—47

6   **Substance**—48
Substance is what wins cases—48
Gear your argument to the standard of review—48
Keep it simple—49
Assume the judges have only a basic familiarity with
    your case unless they show you differently—49
Focus on key facts—50
Strip the authority you use to the bare essentials—52
Minimize the clutter of citations—52
Add a policy argument if you've got a good one—53
Find a theme—54
Pinpoint what was reversible error by the lower
    court—54
Rely on the lower court's opinion if it's well reasoned
    or well written—54
Offer the court an easy way to rule in your favor—55

7   **Structure**—56
Start strong—56
Introduce your argument in a way that is informative,
    interesting, and persuasive—57
After the introduction, move to the facts—59
If you are the appellant, after the facts move to your
    strongest argument—59
If you are the appellee, you must be flexible in
    choosing which argument to start with—60
Give the court signposts—61
Leave time for your conclusion—61
Finish strong—62

8 Questions—64
Questions are gifts—64
Stop talking when a judge asks a question and keep
    quiet until the judge finishes—64
Listen carefully to questions—65
Ask for clarification if you don't understand a
    question—65
Think before you answer—66
Never put off answering a question until later in the
    argument—66
Give a direct answer first, then explain—67
Don't explain too much or too little—68
Disagree with judges gracefully—68
Don't let hypothetical questions push you into
    defending an untenable position—69
Never bluff—69
Flow back into your argument after answering a
    question—70

9 Rebuttal—72
Always reserve rebuttal time—72
Make all your important points in your main
    argument—72
Listen carefully to your opponent's argument—73
Don't waste time on an introduction—73
Clearly connect each point you make to a point you're
    trying to refute—74
If you must repeat something from your main
    argument, say it in a new way—74
Don't try to rebut everything your opponent says—75
Capitalize on unexpected concessions—76
Close quickly—76
Waive your rebuttal time if you don't need it—76

10 Conclusion—77

1 Introduction

This book is for law students and lawyers who want to do well at oral argument. It focuses on how to argue a case before an appellate court. But almost all the advice here applies equally to arguing a motion before a trial court, which most lawyers do more often.

If you're a law student, your first oral argument will come in the spring of your first year, as part of your legal writing course. You will argue orally the arguments you made in an appellate brief. For many of you, this will be your first experience in public speaking. That's why this book starts from scratch. The chapters on nervousness, preparation, and delivery make up a quick course in public speaking.

But you'll need more than public speaking skills to do well at oral argument. An oral argument isn't a speech. In a speech, you talk and the audience listens. In an oral argument, you and your audience interact. The judges decide what you will talk about as much as you do. They can interrupt you with questions at any time. They can cut you off, tell you to move on, or take up your time telling you what they think. And they hold the power to decide your case. The chapters on style, substance, structure, questions, and rebuttal explain the approach you'll need to be effective in this peculiar form of conversation.

Because oral argument is conversational, you can't simply stand before the judges and recite a condensed version of your brief. A brief is like classical music; the notes remain the same no matter what the situation or who's listening. Oral argument is like jazz. It's imperfect, unpredictable, and risky, yet immediate, personal, and powerful. Each oral argument will be different, requiring you to make moment-to-moment adjustments to fit the situation and the judges. To make those adjustments intelligently, you need more than mechanical rules. You need to understand the psychology of persuasion. In this book, I've tried to explain that psychology by giving you the reasons for each suggestion I make. If you understand those reasons, when you're up there all alone—just you and the judges—you'll be able to improvise the music on your own.

2 Nervousness

Oral argument is scary.   Law students and lawyers are competitive. We want to win. We hate to lose. We fear failure. We fear failure in public even more. That's why oral argument is so scary. That's why you're nervous.

You're also nervous because oral argument is a one-shot deal. It's live. You can't go back and revise an oral argument as you can a brief.

If you're a law student facing your first oral argument, you have another source of nervousness: fear of the unknown. This book should help eliminate that. After you've read it you'll know what to expect and what to do.

The mortality rate for oral argument is relatively low. I've seen a thousand students go through their first oral argument and guess what? They survived. So will you. And once you get over the hump of that first one, it's all downhill. Every time you argue, the unknown will decrease and your ability and confidence will increase.

In the meantime, this chapter gives you tips on how to live with your nervousness and suggests several concrete things you can do to reduce it.

Nervousness is normal. Law students aren't the only ones who feel nervous about oral argument. Experienced lawyers feel that way too. In fact, polls show that most people are more afraid of public speaking than of dying. To me this only proves that most people who are polled don't think carefully about the questions.

My point is: you're human.   Don't interpret your nervousness as a personal flaw. Be gentle with yourself.

3

Nervousness is a normal human response to an exciting and scary challenge. It shows you care about your performance or your case. When you stop being nervous, start worrying. You've either stopped caring or stopped breathing.

Controlled nervousness can be useful. Human beings and other animals are programmed to respond to stress by fleeing or fighting. But you're not allowed to run from the courtroom or punch out the judges. You must transform the stress into productive energy. Before your argument, channel it into preparation. During your argument, channel it into performance. Nervous energy is high voltage power. Harness it.

Nervousness usually disappears soon after you start arguing. Athletes nervous before a game usually find that the nervousness disappears as soon as the game starts. The same thing should happen to you once you get past the first minute or so of your argument. That's one reason it's a good idea to memorize your introduction. You can also write it out in full as a crutch. By the time you've finished your introduction, you'll be more relaxed and ready to speak from your outline.

Most nervousness doesn't show. Many students believe their nervousness is obvious when in fact it isn't. You perceive the signs of nervousness as magnified because you're experiencing them from the inside. But only you can hear the blood pounding in your head. On the outside, you look normal.

And even if you look a little nervous, it's not the end of the world. If it's not extreme—like Albert Brooks' nervous sweating in *Broadcast News*—the judges will do their best to ignore it and focus on the substance of your argument. You should do the same.

Most judges want you to do well. In a real case, the judges want you to do well out of self-interest. They have an immediate problem: they must understand and decide your case.

They are looking to you for help. The better your performance, the easier their job.

Judges also want to avoid the discomfort of watching an unsuccessful performer. Nothing makes me more uncomfortable than watching a comedian who isn't funny. The silence of the audience following each joke makes me cringe. I desperately want to avoid vicariously feeling their pain of rejection. Partly for the same reason—and partly out of simple human decency— judges want you to perform well.

In this sense, they're on your side. Keep that in mind as you look up at their faces. They don't want you to stumble over your words, or forget what you were saying, or lose your place. And if you do, they'll probably help you out.

On the other hand, you must be prepared for the occasional nasty judge. Maybe the judge ate the wrong thing for breakfast. Or maybe the judge doesn't like your client or your case and is taking it out on you. Don't take it personally. View it as a personality disorder in the judge and not as a shortcoming in yourself. No matter what happens out there, you're still a good person.

Identify with your client's cause. Nervousness often comes from being too self-conscious. Let concern for the client take your mind off yourself. If your case is only hypothetical, use your imagination. You're a lawyer. A human being has come to your office with a problem. Empathize. Think about your client's cause and the larger legal issues at stake. Get involved.

The more you focus on the client's cause, the easier it is to argue. The cultural rule that we be modest about ourselves doesn't apply when we're talking about another. That's one reason professional athletes and entertainers hire agents. That's also one reason people hire lawyers to argue their cases.

If you're nervous arguing a hypothetical case, be thankful you don't have the fear a lawyer has in a real case: losing the appeal. The lawyer has to answer to the client for failure, and the client has to pay the price in money or liberty. If you fail as a student, the only person who suffers is you. Feeling better already, right?

Get in touch with your body. If you're a first-year law student, this has probably been a rough year for your body. You've spent most of your time sitting: listening to lectures, studying for classes and exams, writing for your legal writing course. After a while, you begin to feel like a disembodied brain.

Maintain balance in your life during this stressful time. Exercise. Play sports. Dance. Walk. Get a massage. Stay in touch with your body. When you give your oral argument, you're going to have to keep it under control.

Relaxation techniques can help. There are lots of them. They include meditation, yoga, and guided imagery. Beer isn't one of them. Find a technique that feels natural and comfortable. Start practicing it right away. The sooner you start, the more likely it will have the desired effect when you need it.

Breathe properly. Many relaxation techniques are based on breathing, which occupies a unique position among bodily functions. It's the only vital unconscious function everyone can consciously control. When you consciously breathe properly you accomplish two things. First, you interrupt the stress response by stopping the chattering of your conscious mind and giving it something productive to do. Second, you start a chain reaction in your unconscious that calms other involuntary functions—such as your heart rate, adrenalin level, and gastrointestinal functions —that you ordinarily can't control.

Proper breathing is also the physical foundation of your voice. Singers and actors train accordingly. All you need to know, however, is how to breathe from your abdomen. When you inhale, your abdomen should expand outward. When you exhale, it should move back in. Make your breaths slow, deep, and rhythmic. If only your chest is expanding and contracting when you breathe, you aren't using your diaphragm correctly.

Chest breathing will make you tight and tense; abdominal breathing will relax you.

Practice breathing properly in the weeks before your oral argument. Feel how it calms and centers you. Do it whenever you feel nervousness interfering with your ability to concentrate. By the time of your argument, proper breathing should be second nature.

Watch as many oral arguments as you can. Your oral argument shouldn't be the first one you see. The earlier you start watching arguments, the earlier your fear of the unknown will disappear. Watch them at an appellate court if there is one in your city. If there isn't, your law school library should have arguments on videotape.

If you watch many oral advocates, you'll see a broad spectrum of styles. This should help you find your own style. You'll also pick up ideas and strategies you can use yourself. And you'll see that even experienced lawyers sometimes stumble over words, or lose their train of thought, or get stumped by a hard question from the bench. Finally, you'll be relieved—and possibly dismayed—to see that most lawyers are not brilliant oral advocates. Most just slog their way through. With a little coaching, preparation, and practice, you can do better.

Visualize success. Athletes preparing for competition commonly use visualization in addition to physical training. While relaxing, they visualize their bodies executing techniques perfectly. This kind of mental rehearsal can work for you too. Visualize yourself arguing and handling questions from the judges well. Then turn the sound off. You can't hear your words, but you can still see yourself standing at the podium, poised and confident. Control your nervousness by rehearsing success. Think positive.

Prepare thoroughly. You can't perform well in oral argument with a positive attitude alone. Your positive attitude must be grounded in reality. You've got to do the work. You've got to put in the time. There's no substitute for preparation. If you're a lawyer, you have an ethical obligation to your client to be prepared.

Start your preparation early. Staying on schedule will help you feel more at ease along the way. When you face the judges, nothing combats nervousness more than knowing your argument cold.

Forget about winging it. Arguing unprepared is like jumping out of a plane without a parachute. You'll make a big impact, but not the kind you want. The next chapter tells you how to be fully prepared.

3 Preparation

Know the record. In a hypothetical case, the record may be merely a short statement of facts and an explanation of the decision by the trial court. But in a real case, the record can be voluminous. It includes transcipts of testimony, documents and other exhibits admitted as evidence at trial, and the opinion of any lower court in your case.

Know what's in the record and where it can be found. You don't have to memorize the entire record, but you should memorize critical testimony and be able to precisely describe other critical evidence. You should also memorize or put a note on your outline where such testimony or other evidence can be found. That way you'll be ready if a judge asks you to point to the place in the record that substantiates your claims about the facts.

Know the law. If your case involves a statute, administrative rule, or constitutional provision, you must know it intimately. You must also know intimately any important case involved in your case. That means you must know the facts and holding, the court that decided the case, and the year the case was decided. Be prepared to give a quick summary of the facts of any important case if a judge asks you to. You don't have to memorize the citation. Citations clutter your argument. They are best left in the brief.

If much time has passed since you wrote your brief—which will always happen in a real case—within a few days of your argument you should quickly update your research. Shepardize the important cases to make sure they're still good. If something important has changed, integrate the new authority into your argument.

Check the court rules to see if there are requirements that must be met before you can argue authority that isn't in your brief. Generally you should send copies of any new authority you intend to use to the court and to your opponent. If the new authority has a radical effect on your case, and there's enough time before your argument, file a written motion with the appellate court asking permission to submit a supplemental memorandum.

If there isn't time to make a written motion or mail out the new authority, bring copies with you to the argument. Hand them to your opponent and to the clerk of court before you argue. When it's your turn to argue, explain the new authority and ask the court whether it wants you to submit a supplemental memorandum.

Know the court. This is simply a particular application of the first rule of public speaking: know your audience. In a student argument, you will rarely know anything specific about your judges. A moot court has no public record of published opinions as a real court does. You only can count on a few characteristics common to most real judges.

Most judges are conservative in their expectations of how lawyers should act in their courtrooms. You will therefore be wise to follow the conventions discussed in this book. Most judges also have a keen sense of legal relevance. They are much less likely than a jury to be swayed by a purely emotional argument.

If you're a lawyer arguing before a real court, study the previously published opinions of the court on the issues involved in your argument. If you know which judges will be hearing your case—as you often will in federal court—check to see whether any of them were involved in deciding a relevant case. Check the law library for articles and seminar publications about oral argument in your jurisdiction. Ask other lawyers about customs of the court and habits of the judges. Find out whether the judges read the briefs before the argument and whether they tend to ask a lot of questions. As much as possible, tailor your argument to fit the court.

Tailoring an argument to fit particular judges is difficult with most appellate courts. Usually you will argue before only a small panel of judges out of the total on the court and you won't know ahead of time which judges will be on the panel. Your ability to tailor the argument to any particular judge will also decrease as the size of the panel increases.

Remember that your audience is not your client. Because clients don't understand the law as well as you do, they don't understand what is relevant as well as you do. They will often want to hear you tell the court about all the bad things the other side did. But you must design your argument to persuade the court, not to please the client. Explain that to your client if your client wants to come to the oral argument.

Know the rules. Each jurisdiction or court may have its own rules. If you don't know the rules for a particular court, call the clerk of court and get them. The most important rule you need to know is exactly how much time you will have to argue. This will determine the nature of your argument more than any other factor.

Know how time is kept and whether you will be signaled how much time is left at certain intervals. Most courts have some kind of light system. Usually a green light is on for most of your argument, a yellow light indicates you only have a certain amount of time left, and a red light indicates your time is up. Check with the clerk to be sure you understand the timing. In many courts, the clerk will customize the timing at your request.

If you're the appellant, you need to know whether the court allows rebuttal. When the court does, you need to know whether it is automatic or must be requested by you.

If you want to use a visual aid—especially one involving a

mechanical device like an overhead projector—you need to know whether the court will allow it and how and when to set it up. Talk to the clerk in advance to make arrangements.

Finally, know where to sit. Changing seats in front of the judges is really embarrassing.

Anticipate questions. You should do more than simply prepare answers to questions you anticipate. You should actually integrate those answers into your planned argument, especially if they concern weaknesses in your case. Weaknesses cannot be hidden. They must be addressed directly in some way that minimizes the harm to your overall position. You will appear stronger and more forthright if you answer questions about weaknesses before they are asked.

A good trial lawyer presenting a witness uses the same principle. If there is some weakness in the witness's testimony, the lawyer will bring it out on direct examination. Volunteered in the proper context, damning facts do less damage.

If the weakness doesn't come out until cross-examination, the context maximizes its damage. Also, the jury may conclude the witness was trying to hide the weakness and may doubt the witness's credibility on testimony that wasn't weak.

So if there's a weakness in your argument, cover it in your presentation, and cover it early so you don't get asked about it before you get to it. Cover any potential question, even if it's not about a weakness in your argument, if you think the judges are likely to ask it. The judges will think you intelligent and considerate for anticipating their questions.

Finally, if there is only a slight chance the judges will ask a question about something, and it's a minor point, prepare an answer just in case it comes up.

Although it's rare to complete an argument without being asked anything by the judges, it can happen. So don't count on questions to get you through your argument. Don't think you can skip preparing an outline because you're only going to get thrown off with questions anyway. Prepare as if you're going to argue all the way through without interruption.

Know your teammate's arguments. Students will often be paired to argue one side of a case as a team. Lawyers argue in teams too, especially in multiparty litigation. When you argue as a team, one of you will handle the facts and you will divide the issues between you. The first to argue should tell the court how you've divided the issues.

Sometimes a judge will forget or ignore how you've divided the issues and ask you a question that concerns one of your teammate's arguments. If you can't answer it, you are put in an awkward situation and your side may lose a golden opportunity. If you answer incorrectly, you force your teammate into the dilemma of whether to contradict you. So learn as much as you can about your teammate's arguments. You won't be able to know them as well as your teammate, but you at least should know the main points.

If you are asked the question before your teammate has argued, start with a disclaimer. Tell the court that the question concerns an issue to be covered by your teammate. Then answer it briefly. If you don't put the disclaimer first, you may be interrupted with another question on the same issue before you get to your disclaimer. The further into the issue you get before making the disclaimer, the more lame it sounds. Putting it first also alerts the judges to save further questions on the issue for your teammate. If you are asked the question after your teammate has finished arguing, skip the disclaimer and answer the question as best you can.

If you are totally unprepared to answer the question, and your teammate hasn't argued yet, you might say: "Your Honor, that question concerns an issue that I am unprepared to argue but that will be argued by my co-counsel. With your permission, I would like to defer to my co-counsel to answer your question." By openly admitting you are unprepared on the issue, you avoid looking like you're evading the question and you may score a point for candor. If the judge accepts your offer, resume your argument. It will then be your teammate's responsibility to answer the question, without counting on or waiting for the judge to ask it again.

If you are totally unprepared to answer the question, and your teammate has already finished arguing, you're probably out of luck. You might offer to submit a supplemental memorandum on the issue, but courts rarely accept such offers. It's also unlikely the court will allow you to sit down and your teammate to come back to the podium to answer the question. More likely, if you can't answer a question, the court will simply ask you to resume your argument, and your side will never get a chance to answer the question.

If your teammate makes an obvious mistake before your turn to argue—such as misstating a fact or an applicable rule of law —you're put in a difficult spot. If the mistake is trivial, for the sake of unity let it go. But if the mistake is significant, correct it when your turn comes. Your teammate shouldn't feel betrayed. You can make the correction gently, in a way that minimizes the damage. If you don't do it, your opponents will. And they won't be so gentle.

Make an outline. As discussed more fully in the next chapter, the correct speaking style for oral argument is conversational. You will neither read nor memorize your argument. To speak in a conversational style without forgetting anything important, you need an outline of your most important points. Some brave souls like to argue without anything in front of them, but that's risky. If you get lost, go blank, or get a brain cramp, you're in deep trouble if you don't have something on paper.

The shorter your outline, the better. Ideally, your entire outline should be in front of you the entire time you're arguing. That means it must fit on a page or two of paper. An open manila folder is ideal because it's thicker than paper and won't rustle.

With your entire outline before you, you'll never have to worry about the distraction of turning a page or shuffling a card. You'll never have to worry about getting pages or cards out of order. And you'll never have to waste time searching frantically for an answer and then—after finding it and giving it—waste more time searching frantically for the place you left off. Your brain is faster than your hand. Having your outline on a page or two means you've taken the time to get most of the argument into your head. This will give you maximum flexibility to follow the judges' questions wherever they might lead.

Not everyone feels comfortable with a short outline. Some people need a detailed outline with every point written on it. Other people don't really *need* a detailed outline, but just don't feel secure without it. If you're either kind of person, do what you need to do. But your goal should be to reduce the size of your outline each time you practice your argument.

If your outline is still several pages long by the time of your argument, don't staple them together or use the top pages of a legal pad. Flipping and folding are noisy and awkward. Keep pages separate so you can slide them gracefully from top to bottom. For simplicity, consider putting each issue on a separate page.

If your outline is long, don't try to get it all in front of you by writing smaller. Write your outline in big thick letters so you can see your words without straining even if the podium is too low or the lighting is poor. Highlight or underline key words and critical points.

You can even color code your outline. There are lots of ways to do this. You could have legal points in one color, factual points in another, and case names and references to the record in another. Or you could have main points in one color and subpoints in another. Or you could have each issue in a different color.

One handy technique is to use half of an open manila folder for your outline and the other half for summaries of cases. Write the summaries on cards. On the bottom line of each card, write the name of the case. Tape them to the left side of the folder, one on top of the other in alphabetical order, with just the bottom line of each showing. If you get a question that requires you to refresh your memory about a particular case, just flip to the appropriate card. You can also use cards arranged in this way to refresh your memory about other authorities or facts.

If your outline won't fit on the right half of the folder, tape the cards to a separate piece of cardboard and lay them next to your outline on the podium. If your outline won't fit on both sides of the folder and you need to use several pages, keep the cards on the left side of the folder and lay the pages of your outline on the right.

Your outline should have the main points written on the left side of the page. Subpoints go under each main point and start slightly to the right of each main point. Sub-subpoints go under each subpoint and start even further to the right. The amount of time you have will determine how far to the right you get under any main point.

If you want to focus on a particular aspect of your delivery, your outline can remind you of it. For example, if you tend to speak too fast, you could write "**SLOW**" in big bold letters at the top of your outline. Every time you look down you'll be reminded to speak slowly. But try this first in practice to make sure your reminder isn't more distracting than helpful.

On the next page is a sample one-page outline of an argument. You don't need to understand its substance. Just examine its form.

Plan what you will bring to the podium. You aren't going to bring much with you. The main thing you need is your outline. You may want to bring your brief in case a judge asks you something that requires you to refer to it. You can bring all the briefs if they aren't too thick. If the record is less than about two inches thick you can bring that too, or you can photocopy pages that might be the subject of specific questions. Index the briefs and record with something like yellow Post-it notes so you can find things fast.

Intro

~~Facts~~
  Bates admits <u>no settlement</u>
    (letter 3/18/91)
  Night before: "releases all around" (Tr.I7)
  Hallway: "until the end of the world"
    (Tr. I-49)
  Courtroom: "all claims" (Stip. p.8)
  * Chen heard <u>what she expected</u>
      <u>to hear</u>
  Objected later that same day
    (letter 3/29/91)

Court has <u>great discretion</u> (<u>Anderson</u>)
  <u>Mistake</u> good grounds (Tomscak)

  Four factors:
    Competence?
    extensive negotiations?
   ⌈Party agree in open court?
   ⌊Party questioned by judge?
    ⌐> Dahl <u>not</u> in courtroom *

  <u>Glorvigen</u> (438 N.W.2d 692)
    Party's presence critical when:
      1. last-minute negotiations
      2. not reduced to writing

  distinguish <u>Beach</u>:
      1. extensive negotiations
      2. reliance
      3. delay
Conclusion: Rescission <u>equitable</u>

Arrange what you bring neatly. If the podium has a shelf, put everything except your outline on it. Don't clutter the podium.

Nine times out of ten, you won't have to refer to the briefs or the record during an argument. So if you feel burdened having all those documents with you at the podium, leave them at the counsel table, especially if the table is within easy reach of the podium. There's a certain lean, clean feeling you get when you walk to the podium with only an outline in your hand. That feeling may be worth the risk you'll have to reach over to the counsel table for a brief or transcript.

If you're arguing someplace other than an appellate courtroom, with nothing and no one to signal the time to you, you'll need to bring a watch to the podium. Don't bring a digital watch that can only be read from a certain angle. Take the watch off your wrist before you walk to the podium. When you get to the podium, inconspicuously lay it next to your outline where you can see it easily.

Don't take water with you to the podium. If your mouth is dry, before the argument starts pour yourself a glass of water at the counsel table and leave it there. Don't try pouring water after the argument has begun. Your hands will be less steady and a mishap would be disastrous. A friend once spilled water all over the counsel table and the court had to stop the argument so the clerk could wipe it up. Arguing from a soggy outline was no fun.

Think twice before using a visual aid in an appellate court. You may know about studies showing we remember something twice as well if we both hear it and see it than if we only hear it or see it alone. But in most appellate arguments you're not going to be able to use this finding to your advantage. Although visual aids are common and easy to use in trial courts, in appellate courts they generally create more problems than they're worth.

The first problem is that visual aids have not traditionally been used in appellate courts. Most appellate judges are either conservative by nature or are made conservative by a life lived under the principle of stare decisis. They are comfortable with the way things have always been in their courtrooms. A visual aid rocks their boat.

The second problem is that visual aids take time to set up. That time may be deducted from the time you have to argue. When you only have twenty minutes, every one is precious.

The third problem is that visual aids can be undependable. This isn't much of a problem if you have plenty of time to set one up and test it out in a trial court. But in an appellate court you often won't be able to set up your visual aid until immediately before you argue. Even if it's something as simple as a large diagram or photograph on posterboard, it can fall off the stand when you try to set it up in a hurry.

The fourth problem is that it's hard to place a visual aid where everyone can see it. Often your opponents are beside the podium at a counsel table, while the judges are in front of the podium. A compromise position for the visual aid may make it hard for everyone to see.

The fifth problem is that a visual aid can be distracting. It can distract the judges, who may choose to look at it when you would prefer they look at you. Even when the judges look at a visual aid at the right time, it interrupts the person-to-person contact that is one of your most powerful tools of persuasion. A visual aid can also distract you. Handling the mechanical tasks associated with presenting a visual aid is just one more thing to worry about at a time when you've already got plenty on your mind.

Despite the potential problems, you still may decide a visual aid is essential to your argument. Use one if it is more clear or compelling than your words alone could possibly be. For example, your words alone may not be as compelling as a photograph of the scene of the crime. Or you may have a complex factual pattern that becomes much clearer when presented on a chart.

Your visual aid will usually be an object, photograph, or document used as a trial exhibit. But sometimes a visual aid created specifically for oral argument is helpful, like a chart showing the complex relationship between several parties or a complex procedural history. When you create a visual aid, make it as simple as possible so it's immediately understandable. Remember: the clock is running.

Pick the easiest way to present your visual aid. Keep the technology simple. Choose the method with the fewest possible things that can go wrong. The simplest and easiest visual aid to use is a blown-up document, diagram, or photograph on a piece of posterboard. Make sure it's large enough. Words or numbers should be two inches tall to be easily readable from twenty to thirty feet.

Keep the posterboard near the podium until you need it, then put it on a stand. Don't count on the court's having a stand; bring your own. Only hold it up by hand if you have no other choice. If you hold it, every time you move, it will move too. Never turn your back to the judges while using it. Never talk while looking at it.

When you're done with the posterboard, take it down or cover it before continuing with your argument. Leave it visible only if the image is more compelling than anything you have left to say.

If you want to use an overhead projector or some other mechanical device, get the court's permission in advance. Check out the courtroom so you know exactly where and how you're going to set up the device. Some courts require you to set it up before the first argument of the day has begun. If you're going to have to set it up immediately before you argue, practice setting it up in a hurry. If your teammate is going to help you set it up, practice together. If you're using a projector, bring an extension cord and a spare bulb. Prepare for anything that might go wrong. If something unexpected happens, be prepared to argue without your visual aid.

Perfect your writing. The martial artist practices endlessly in slow motion. Only then can the master properly attend to the details of the art. Writing is slow-motion practice in the art of verbal expression. Through careful work on your writing, you can learn to express yourself with clarity, grace, and power. Practice the techniques of good legal writing until they are a part of you. Make them automatic. When you face the judges, and must construct your sentences quickly under pressure, the right words will come.

Practice your argument. The more you practice your argument, the better. And the more the conditions you practice under resemble the conditions of the actual argument, the better. Start by going through your argument in any quiet, peaceful spot where you feel comfortable. At some point, you may want do it in a mirror to see how you look. Start with the bathroom mirror with the door closed. Your voice will sound great resonating off the tiles. Then work your way up to mirrors in more dignified rooms.

But trying to concentrate on arguing and observing yourself at the same time can mean you'll do neither very well. That's why watching yourself arguing on videotape is better than simply practicing in the mirror. Videotape is the best tool for analyzing your delivery and for becoming aware of any annoying or distracting mannerisms you may have.

You'll be amazed at what you see, just as you were amazed the first time you heard your voice on tape. When I'm videotaped with a group, I'm always amazed at how all the people look like themselves except me. I always assume there was a small defect on the part of the lens pointed at me.

Practice your argument all the way through each time. Don't start over from the beginning every time you get lost or make a mistake. If you do, your "May it please the court" will be dynamite, but you'll never make it to your conclusion. Doing the entire argument each time means no part will be neglected.

Time your entire argument. Try to make your uninterrupted argument take up about 80 percent of the time you have to argue. But remember that when you give it for real it will almost certainly be shorter or longer than it was in practice. Add a little nervous energy and you're done five minutes early. Add a few questions from the judges and five minutes out of your twenty are gone. Plan where you will cut corners if you need to.

When you feel you're ready, practice in front of people. Pick people you would be embarrassed to look foolish in front of who are capable of understanding your argument. Friends from law school often fall in this category. They can act like judges, questioning you on your position and forcing you to think on your feet. Friends who aren't working on the same case will be in a position similar to the judges. Because they will have a fresh view of the case, they are likely to think of questions you didn't anticipate.

Take this practice before friends seriously. Make it as realistic as possible. Don't crack jokes or take time-outs. Stay in character. When you're done, invite their comments. Promise you'll remain friends no matter what they say, and keep your promise.

Your friends will probably make you more nervous than the real judges, because nobody likes to look like a fool in front of friends. Baseball pitchers sometimes pitch with a grapefruit the day before a big game, so the ball will seem small and manageable by comparison. After arguing before your friends, arguing before the judges will seem easy by comparison.

Check out the courtroom. This is another way to calm your nerves. Make the unknown known. Familiarity breeds comfort.

Visit the courtroom at least a day before your argument. Watch some arguments to get a feel for the judges and the protocol.

If you can, also check out the courtroom when it's empty. Stand at the podium. See how it feels. Talk a little. Test the acoustics of the room. If there's a microphone, check to see whether it's the right height. If it's not, practice adjusting it. Check to see whether the podium is adjustable. Hang around until you feel comfortable. When you come back to argue, the courtroom will feel like home.

Give yourself a break. Finish your preparation by dinnertime the day before your argument. That will leave you the evening to take a break. Taking a break allows you to rest while your subconscious absorbs and integrates your argument. If you've prepared properly, this will do you more good than reading the cases one more time. Do something to take your mind off the next day's argument. Go to a movie, wash your feet, reconcile quantum physics with relativity theory—whatever distracts you. Then get a good night's sleep. If you're like me, you'll dream you're arguing before the court in your underwear.

On the day of your argument, go over it one last time. Eat lightly. A heavy meal will draw blood to your stomach and make you tired. Avoid drinking a lot of liquid; you don't want to feel like you have to go to the bathroom during your argument. Unless you're an addict, avoid alcohol and caffeine. You're going to need all the brain cells you have for this experience.

Arrive at the courtroom early. Respect Murphy's Law. Your dog may chew up your outline, you may spill something on your clothes, you may have trouble finding a parking place, the courtroom may not be where you left it. Only if you allow enough time to arrive at the courtroom early will you have time to deal with unexpected problems.

If nothing goes wrong, you'll arrive at the courtroom with time to spare. Take that time to run through your outline one last time. Assemble your thoughts. Summon your powers. Center yourself. You're ready.

4 Style

You can't be totally yourself. Many experts on oral argument advise you to "be yourself." That's fine if you naturally are at ease speaking in public, naturally possess a strong, confident, respectful-yet-conversational speaking style, naturally use effective gestures, facial expressions, and vocal dynamics, and naturally are free of distracting vocal and bodily mannerisms when you speak. If you're not a natural, then study and practice the techniques in this chapter and the next.

When you've mastered these techniques, you won't have to think about them when you argue. They will be stored in your subconscious. A guitarist practices scales over and over, weaving them into the nerve pathways between brain and hand. When it's time to play a solo, the hands take care of themselves, leaving the guitarist free to concentrate on the music. When you've mastered the necessary techniques, you'll be able to concentrate on the music of your argument. The less your conscious mind is burdened with matters of form when you're at the podium, the more you'll be free to concentrate on substance.

Don't follow the techniques in this book slavishly. Adapt them to your personality. Build on your natural strengths. Don't mimic someone else's personal style. Become a more polished version of yourself.

Speak in a conversational style. Don't give a speech to the judges. A speech is something you created alone. A conversation is something you create together. If you create something together, you form a relationship. Conversation creates relationship, and our relationships largely determine our judgments about people and our willingness to help them.

Forced to choose, I will help my sister or brother before my friend, my friend before a stranger. If you can create a relationship between you and the judges, no matter how tenuous, you will increase the chances they will trust you and want to help you.

Of course, you can't force the judges to converse with you. But you can create the illusion of conversation by speaking in a conversational style. Using this style makes each judge feel you are talking to him or her individually. It makes you seem accessible. It invites conversation.

Hopefully the judges will accept your invitation and start asking you questions. The illusion of conversation will then become a reality. Once real conversation starts, cement your relationship with the judges by showing flexibility in your presentation. Listen when a judge asks a question. Adjust what you say to match the level of understanding revealed by the question. Watch for nonverbal cues from the judges, just as you would in any normal conversation. Nodding of the head shows agreement. Shaking of the head shows disagreement. Rolling of the eyes shows boredom or disbelief. Respond to those cues.

Conversational style comes partly through technique, but more important than technique is attitude. When you argue, talk as if you are sitting around a table with the judges. In real life, judges usually meet twice as a group to consider a case. One of those times is the oral argument. Think of your argument as a chance to sit in on their meeting, a chance to help them understand the case and make the right decision. Talk *with* the judges, not *at* them. Respectfully explain, never lecture. You want to be at the table, not on the menu.

Use plain English. Plain English is language that is simple, clear, direct, precise, and concise. It's the writing style now universally recommended in legal writing texts and courses. Since the ear has more difficulty following a legal argument than the eye, speaking plain English is even more important than writing it. The short sentences you wrote in your brief should be even shorter in your oral argument. You can also use contractions, which are inappropriate in formal legal writing. These will help your oral argument sound more natural and conversational than your brief.

But plain English doesn't mean sloppy English. You probably speak simply and directly, but speaking clearly, precisely, and concisely takes practice and concentration. It also takes mastery of the subject matter of your argument. Where your thinking is unclear, your language will be unclear.

The language you use in oral argument can be less formal than that of a written argument. But there are limits. When you answer a question, say "yes," not "yeah." Avoid slang. Say the defendant was "drunk," not "smashed."

Avoid obscenities. Even if an obscenity is important in the facts, hearing the word aloud will make the judges uncomfortable. You may hope to show that the opposing party was bad for saying a dirty word, but if you repeat it some of the dirt will rub off on you. So refer to an obscenity indirectly. Don't spell out the word; you'll sound infantile. Just say: "Massey was about to walk away when the defendant shouted an obscenity at him." If the judges are really interested, they can look up the actual word in your brief.

Your language can be more vivid and colorful than that in a written argument. But don't exaggerate. Avoid unwarranted superlatives. Don't label every opposing argument "frivolous" or "outrageous." Never use language that makes you appear unreasonable.

Avoid "I statements" in the body of your argument. You can use first-person pronouns when you're introducing yourself, your teammate, and your argument. For example, you can say: "I will show that the statute was never intended to cover the defendant's conduct." But once you get into the body of your argument, take yourself out of your sentences. Don't say "In my opinion," "I believe," "I think," or—worst of all—"I feel." These make your arguments sound subjective. Strictly speaking, what you as an individual believe or think isn't legally relevant. The judges want to know the facts and the law and how the law applies to the facts. Structure your sentences to give them only that. Make yourself grammatically invisible in your argument.

Omit introductory phrases that weaken your arguments. If you represent Stoltz, don't introduce your arguments with phrases such as "Stoltz maintains," "Stoltz contends," or "Stoltz argues." Introductory words that label what you're saying as a mere argument are not only needless, but actually harmful. They imply there are two plausible positions on the issue. What you want to imply is that there is only one correct view of your case.

So don't say "Stoltz maintains the light was red." Say "The evidence shows the light was red." Don't say "Stoltz contends the contract was unconscionable." Say "The contract was unconscionable." In your introduction, don't say "I will argue the statute is not applicable in this case." Say "I will show the statute is not applicable in this case." Present your arguments as reality. Use phrases containing "maintains," "contends," or "argues" only when you're talking about the other side's arguments.

Show respect for the court without fawning. You show proper respect for the court by following the conventions that signify respect. Stand when you speak to the court, even if it is to answer a single question before you've begun your argument. Stop talking when a judge interrupts your argument to ask you a question. Keep quiet until the judge finishes the question. Avoid jokes and slang. Be serious and dignified.

Address a single judge as "Your Honor." Don't use "Sir" or "Ma'am." Address the court as "the court" or "this court." Address more than one judge as "Your Honors." You can also use "Your Honors" to address the entire court. When referring to earlier decisions in your case, avoid the vague phrase "the lower court." Instead, be specific: "the trial court," "the district court," "the court of appeals."

Avoid phrases that might offend the court. Tell the court what it *should* do, not what it *must* do. Don't be pushy. In answer to a question, don't say "as I said before" even if you have said something before. The judge who asked the question may take it to imply "You should have been listening the first time" or "You should have understood it the first time, you dummy."

You avoid fawning by not overdoing the conventions that show respect. You may start an answer to a judge's question with "Your Honor," but if you get a series of short questions, don't start every answer with it. Don't seek the court's permission for every trivial act. If you're at the podium and a judge's question requires that you walk a couple steps to your counsel table to grab a volume of the transcript, don't ask the court's permission.

Even if you know a judge's name, it's better to address the judge as "Your Honor" when answering a question from that judge. Addressing the judge as "Judge So-and-so" can make you seem overfamiliar or obsequious.

But referring to a judge by name can be an effective technique when you are answering a question from *another* judge: "As Justice So-and-so pointed out earlier . . ." or "As Judge So-and-so pointed out in his opinion in *Chatlos*. . . ." This enlists the judge referred to in support of your argument and draws that judge in. Just be sure you know the correct name and title of any judge you refer to. That's no problem if the judges have nameplates in front of them, but you still have to make sure you get the pronunciation right.

Don't fall all over yourself talking about how brilliant a judge's comment, question, or opinion was. Don't add flattering adjectives when referring to a judge—whether the judge is on the court hearing your case or another court—as in "the learned Judge So-and-so" or "the honorable Judge So-and-so." Don't do it when you address or refer to the court either, as in "this learned court" or "this honorable court."

A lawyer who offers doughnuts to the judges is a lawyer with a weak case. Do not attempt to curry favor with the court. Appear respectful and no more.

Refer to the opposing party, not the opposing advocate. Avoid giving the other side air time during your argument. As much as possible, present your arguments without reference to the other side's arguments. When you must refute an argument directly, put it into the mouth of the opposing party, not the opposing advocate: "IBM's argument overlooks this court's holding in the *Chatlos* case," not "My opponent's argument overlooks this court's holding in the *Chatlos* case."

Referring to the opposing party helps you avoid appearing to make an unseemly personal attack on the opposing advocate. Your terminology also implies the opposing party is responsible for all arguments made by the lawyer. This prevents the judges from minimizing a flaw in the opposing party's argument by attributing it to lawyer error.

Refer to the parties the same way you did in your brief. Don't risk confusing the court by changing what you call them in your oral argument. When you're writing your brief, carefully consider what to call the parties. Usually it's best to refer to them by name. This helps make the facts of your case clear and vivid, and helps make your client come alive to the court. If you have several clients, try to find some descriptive name for them, such as "the tenants" or "the shareholders," rather than using their litigation roles, such as "the defendants" or "the appellants."

If you can't help acknowledging the opposing advocate as a human being, you have several choices. You can say "my opponent" or "my adversary." You can say "opposing counsel." You can include the litigation role, as in "counsel for appellant" or "counsel for defendant." Or you can include the name of the party, as in "counsel for IBM" or "counsel for Smith." If you use one of these, use it consistently. Don't switch around.

Avoid referring to an opposing advocate by name. Never refer to an opposing advocate by first name, even if you're close friends. And never add flattering adjectives, as in "my learned opponent" or "my worthy opponent." It sounds phony and may even come off as sarcastic.

Another phrase you should avoid is "my client." It emphasizes the purely professional nature of the relationship. It calls attention to the fact that you are arguing because you are being paid to argue. What you want to convey is that you so believe in the rightness of your client's cause, you would argue the case for free. So stick with your client's name.

Call your teammate your "co-counsel." Students arguing as a team should refer to each other as "co-counsel": "My co-counsel, Paul Stoltz, will show the statute doesn't apply." "My colleague" is vague but acceptable. "My associate" doesn't work. Law firms have traditionally been divided between partners (masters) and associates (slaves). Calling your teammate your "associate" implies you are your teammate's boss.

"Co-counsel" is only technically correct if the advocates are representing the same party. When two or more attorneys representing different parties argue as a team, they can simply refer to each other by name: "My name is Alan Dworsky, and I represent appellant Sports Traders. With me is Susan Andrews, representing appellant Market Managers." Or each can refer to the other by the name of the party represented by the other: "My name is Alan Dworsky and I represent appellant Sports Traders. Sports Traders has adopted the arguments on liability made by appellant Market Managers."

Get serious. You can't expect the court to take your case seriously if you don't show that you do. Never tell a planned joke. Avoid spontaneous jokes too. But if the perfect joke or play on words falls in your lap because of a judge's question or comment, you can give in to temptation as long as you resume your serious demeanor immediately afterward. And if a judge cracks a joke, laugh. Otherwise, stay serious.

Show appropriate emotion. Emotion has a place in oral argument. After all, judges are human beings. But arguing before judges is different from arguing before a jury. Judges are more sophisticated than juries in analyzing the arguments of lawyers. They hear lawyers arguing cases day after day. They understand the law and develop a keen sense of legal relevance. They can easily spot a cheap appeal to emotion.

Displays of emotion must be justified. If you claim the police beat your client in the back room of the station house, you can and should show more emotion than if you claim your client was wrongfully denied diversity jurisdiction in the federal courts. Indeed, your character might be suspect if you showed no emotion while claiming your client had been beaten. And if you get all worked up over a procedural technicality, you will appear insincere.

When you have an argument that on its surface does not inspire emotion—like one involving a procedural technicality— dig deeper. Search for underlying policies that might serve as wellsprings for genuine emotion. When you tap into that deeper source, you'll have something to get excited about.

But no matter how justified your emotion, you must keep it under control. Crying, shouting, and fist-pounding are taboo. Emotion has no officially recognized place in the appellate process. It plays a larger role in oral argument than in written briefs, probably because the spoken word is inherently more dramatic. But emotion still plays a minor supporting role to reason. The actors in the drama of oral argument must not undermine the myth that appellate decision-making is a purely rational process. They must help maintain the fiction that rules are applied to facts with mathematical logic in an equation that equals justice.

Obvious expressions of emotion must therefore be limited. But emotion can still be smuggled into your argument. Some can be hidden in the way you order the facts. Some can be concealed in your choice of words. And your voice, face, and body can covertly send all sorts of nonverbal messages. Great oral advocates are masters at smuggling contraband emotion into the courtroom.

If you want to play the game of oral argument, remember the rules. Appear to be appealing solely to the minds of the judges when you are secretly reaching for their hearts.

Convey that you believe in your client's cause. Conveying you believe in your client's cause is important because it addresses unspoken assumptions judges make in a real case. They know that you know more about your case than they do. They know you don't have space in the briefs or time in the argument to tell them all you know. And they assume there are things you cannot tell them, things that never even came out at the trial of the case. Showing your personal commitment to your client's cause gives the judges the subliminal message that if they knew as much as you did, they'd be convinced of the rightness of your client's cause.

You can convey you believe in your client's cause even in cases where you must distance yourself from what your client has done. For example, assume your client has been convicted of some horrible crime. Your argument is that the conviction should be overturned because the police violated your client's constitutional rights. You will cement your relationship with the judges by showing you share their repugnance for the crime. In this situation, root your conviction in the sacredness of the constitutional right. Only in an extreme case—such as when you are representing a serial killer—should you distance yourself from your client as a person.

Following the advice in this chapter will help you convey your belief in your client's cause. Maintain a serious demeanor. Show appropriate emotion. Stay in character. Call your client by name. Ignore minor distractions. Avoid an air of intellectual detachment.

But nothing will help you more to convey your belief in your client's cause than real conviction. Get inside your client's skin. Make the fundamental principles in your case your own. If your argument seems genuine and valuable to you, you won't have to sell it to the judges. They'll want to steal it from you.

Don't break character. If you really believe in your client's cause, staying in character won't be a problem; your self and your role will be one. But if you're using technique to compensate for a lack of conviction, remember that technique is effective only as long as it remains hidden.

Don't do anything to make the judges aware they are watching a performance. When you break character—even for an instant—what looked like conviction will look like an act. "Pay no attention to that man behind the curtain" didn't work for the Wizard. If you work behind a curtain, keep it drawn.

Breaking character can happen in subtle ways. The nervous laugh, the word muttered under your breath in self-reprimand, the gaze upward as you try to remember what you were saying, the sly smile that slips across your face when you're caught in an inconsistency—all make you look like you've messed up your part in a play.

Sometimes a judge will invite you to break character by asking a question like: "Counsel, what do you *really* think?" Don't bite at the bait. Don't let a judge drive a wedge between you and your role. Respond by briefly repeating your argument, perhaps in more personal terms. Convey that what you're arguing and what you really think are one and the same. If you don't act like you believe your argument, you can't expect the court to believe it.

There's no backstage. Acting inappropriately while you aren't arguing can hurt your effectiveness as much as acting inappropriately while you are. Your argument begins the moment you enter the courtroom. Assume the judges are watching everything you do. If your underwear needs adjustment, it will just have to wait.

While you're waiting for the argument to start, don't joke around with your teammate or opponents. While your opponents are arguing, don't visibly communicate with your team-mate. Keep still. Sit straight. Don't slouch. Lean slightly forward. Convey that you are listening respectfully.

When the court signals that it's your turn to argue, stand quickly and head for the podium. Don't drag your feet. Look eager.

When your teammate is arguing, don't pass notes up to the podium or whisper advice. You may have to save that perfect answer for the ride home in the car.

Even when you aren't aware of it, the judges or the court staff may be watching you or listening to you. Judges' clerks often sit in the same area of the courtroom as the attorneys who are waiting for their turn to argue. If you make an inappropriate remark, it may be overheard by the clerk who's going to be writing the opinion in your case. Also, many modern appellate courtrooms are equipped with closed-circuit TV systems, mainly for security purposes. They are used by judges or court staff to watch particular oral arguments from their offices. But the judges or court staff may occasionally use them simply to check on what's going on in the courtroom. Don't be caught doing impressions of the judges or slipping souvenirs from the courtroom into your briefcase.

You must be careful even outside the courtroom. That may be a judge behind you in the elevator or in the next stall.

Deal calmly with distractions. When people are arguing about something important to them, they aren't easily distracted. When my wife and I have one of our rare arguments, an earthquake could hit and we wouldn't break stride. We aren't even distracted by things we should be distracted by, like the cutting stares of the other people at the restaurant who are trying to enjoy their meals. True conviction narrows and intensifies the advocate's focus. If you are easily distracted while arguing, it can be a sign to the judges that you're not really committed to your argument.

But commitment to your argument must be balanced by

concern for your audience. While you cannot allow yourself to be easily distracted, you must show sensitivity to anything that might be distracting to the judges. Be committed but not oblivious.

If a distraction is small, just keep going. For example, someone noisily entering the courtroom shouldn't throw you off. As long as the judges can still hear you, mentally brush the distraction aside as you would a fly buzzing by your head. If a distraction is large, stop and wait until it's over. For example, if a plane flies overhead and the judges can't hear what you're saying, stop talking and wait patiently for it to pass.

If a distraction persists, ask the judges whether they would like you to stop until the problem is corrected. For example, if the courtroom microphone keeps feeding back, tell the judges: "If this noise is distracting to the court, I'd be happy to stop until the problem is corrected."

The most disconcerting distractions are those caused by the judges themselves. For example, a judge may page through a brief or talk to a clerk while you are arguing. When a judge is obviously not listening to your argument, it's usually best to turn your attention to the other judges and just keep going. If you stop talking and wait for the judge to listen, the court might interpret your silence as criticism and consider you insolent.

If two judges are talking to each other, or if no judge is listening to you, your dilemma is tougher. You might look down at your outline and pretend you've come to a natural pause in your argument. Pretend to be busy until the judges are listening again.

Regardless of the source, intensity, and persistence of the distraction, you must keep your cool. Deal with it calmly. Concentrate.

Don't get down in the dirt with your opponent. Attack arguments, not advocates. Judges don't like to see lawyers behaving disrespectfully to each other. Judges are the parents of the court, and it embarrasses them when their children misbehave in public. The Mace you spray will blow back in your face. If your opponent misstates the law or the facts, respond respectfully when it's your turn to argue. Don't mime indignation from your chair. Don't roll your eyes or shake your head. Don't slam down your pen. If your opponent makes scandalous remarks about you or your client, don't respond in kind when it's your turn to argue. Stay above it all. Let the wind do its work.

5 Delivery

Wear appropriate clothes. The ritual of oral argument involves ritual clothing. Oral arguments aren't won by Elvis impersonators. Convention—usually reinforced by court rules—requires professional dress. Although professional dress is largely standardized throughout the country, it can vary from place to place. Find out what's considered appropriate in your court.

For men, professional dress is rigidly defined by tradition. Most men wear dark or gray suits and white, light blue, or pastel shirts with ties. Bright colors are allowed only in ties, but even ties shouldn't be gaudy. Most men choose neckties and consider the bow tie an old-fashioned affectation lacking strength. Perhaps the few men who prefer the bow tie—like Orville Redenbacher—wear it to signify an adherence to old-fashioned values and virtues.

For women, professional dress is less rigidly defined and tends to vary more from place to place. Most women wear suits consisting of a skirt, blouse, and jacket, but conservative dresses are also acceptable. The rules about color are the same as for men. Floral prints are for the beach, not the bench.

Wear comfortable shoes. No sense in having two extra opponents on your feet. Women should wear closed-toed shoes and plain hose. Jewelry should be simple. Avoid anything that dangles, clatters, or glistens.

Learn the nonverbal signals sent by particular items, colors, and styles of clothing. Use extreme caution when following fads; signals can change rapidly as a fad fades. My yellow power tie is now a bridle for my daughter's rocking horse.

Pay attention to detail. Judges spend long hours in windowless courtrooms. They are sensitive to subtle changes in an otherwise monotonous visual field. Make sure they notice what you want them to notice. Check yourself in the mirror carefully before you enter the courtroom.

The guiding principle of dressing for oral argument is not to wear anything that draws attention to itself or your body. The body symbolizes passion, which must not corrupt the rational process of legal decision making. The judges' robes reflect this denial of the body by completely hiding it. The suit worn by lawyers is only slightly less of a camouflage. You are allowed to use gestures to reinforce your words, but you are not allowed to use your body's beauty to influence the judges.

Wear a conservative hairstyle. Like appropriate dress, a conservative hairstyle inspires confidence in the judges, who tend to trust people who look like them. I once saw a woman on *People's Court* argue her case in front of 40 million viewers with curlers in her hair. She didn't inspire confidence. She must have had somewhere pretty important to go after the show.

At least wear your hair so it doesn't fall in your face. Constantly brushing hair out of your eyes or pulling it out of your mouth will distract both you and the judges. If you've got long hair that might get in the way, tie it back or up.

If you like to wear your hair in an unorthodox style, the issue of whether to alter it for your oral argument may be the first identity crisis of your legal career. But an unorthodox hairstyle is not an insurmountable handicap. Look at Einstein. You can usually overcome any bad first impressions with a solid argument and good delivery. But if you're in love with your purple, spiked Mohawk—and you're not an Einstein—you might want to reconsider your choice of careers.

Stand straight. Your stance should be as solid as your argument. Face the judges squarely, with legs straight and both feet planted firmly on the floor about shoulder-width apart.

Keep your head up and your back straight. An upright stance suggests honesty and strength. Don't rock backward and forward like an Orthodox Jew in prayer or sway from side to side like a deck passenger on a ship. Don't drape yourself over the podium, as if you'd collapse without support.

Don't pace. Don't even move from your spot behind the podium unless it's for a specific purpose. Stand your ground.

Rest your hands on the podium. Clasping your hands in front of you in the fig-leaf posture looks silly. Clasping them behind your back makes you look like you're facing a firing squad. Putting them in your pockets looks too informal and may be seen as disrespectful. Putting them on your hips looks confrontational. Putting them in your armpits behind folded arms looks cold and distant. Holding your arms straight at your sides looks relaxed, but it shares a disadvantage with all these other postures: Your hands are down low or tied up, with a long way to travel if you need them to do something on the podium or in the air.

In oral argument, the podium is the most functional place to put your hands. Up there they are always ready when you need them to turn a page or reinforce your words with a gesture. Rest your hands there gently. Don't grip the podium as if you were hanging on for dear life. Don't put your body weight on the podium by leaning on your elbows or forearms; this looks lazy and disrespectful.

Don't fidget with your hands or bring objects to the podium you might be tempted to fidget with. Leave your pencil or pen at the counsel table. You won't be writing during your argument. Empty your pockets of keys and coins before you argue. Then if your hands abandon you at some point and duck into your pockets for cover, at least they won't find anything there to play with. Buy glasses with frames that fit so you aren't constantly pushing them up. Don't hold your outline. This will only inhibit your gestures and magnify any slight tremor in your hands.

If there's no podium and you must argue from behind a table, hold your hands together in front of you at stomach level, with fingertips gently touching or fingers loosely clasped. Otherwise you can hold your hands at your sides, but this makes gesturing more awkward and may make you look like the Tin Man between gestures.

Reinforce your words with gestures. Gestures vary as much as individuals. The main point is that they should look and feel natural. Don't force them.

Use gestures to emphasize important points. Don't gesture constantly. You can take off your glasses to punctuate a dramatic moment, but don't keep taking them off and putting them on throughout your argument. Constant emphasis emphasizes nothing.

Keep your gestures under control. Don't look like you're in the ground crew waving a jet into a terminal. Exaggeration will backfire, damaging your credibility.

Avoid any gesture that could be seen as threatening. Don't pound the podium. Don't point or shake your finger at the judges.

Reinforce your words with facial expressions. Your basic facial expression should be serious but animated. Although smiling is usually a way we show strangers we mean well, it doesn't work as a staple in oral argument. The judges are aware of your role as seller of your argument and will be skeptical of the sincerity of a constant smile. Or they may interpret it as an impertinent assumption of familiarity where none exists. Smiling briefly and occasionally is fine if you do it at appropriate moments. But an appeal is serious business and your face should reflect that.

Being serious is different from being somber. Although an oral argument isn't a party, it isn't a funeral either. When the only thing moving on your face is your mouth, you look dead. Put some energy into your face. Open it up by raising your eyebrows. Make it work with your words. Look alive.

Maintain eye contact with the judges. Eye contact helps you maintain a relationship with the listener and keep the listener's attention. Lack of eye contact is interpreted as a sign that you have something to hide. Would you buy a used car from someone who couldn't look you in the eye?

Give each judge a fair share of your eye contact so none feels slighted. Switch from one judge to another before eye contact crosses the borderline and becomes a threatening stare. An average of three seconds per judge is about right. But don't switch eye contact mechanically from judge to judge. You don't want to look like a talking metronome. Mix it up.

If a judge asks you a question, you should maintain eye contact with that judge at least during the beginning of your answer. As your answer branches out, your eye contact can branch out to other judges. If you do maintain eye contact with the questioning judge during your entire answer, breaking eye contact can serve as a sign that you have finished your answer and moved back into your argument.

Finally, if you perceive that one judge is particularly resistant to your argument, make eye contact with that judge when you make an especially persuasive point. It may be your only hope of getting through.

Don't read your argument. Reading prevents you from forming a relationship with the judges. You can't maintain eye contact or create the illusion of conversation. The judges may even think you rude or ill-prepared. Reading also denies you the flexibility essential to effective argument. As soon as the judges start asking questions, your script will be useless and you will be lost. Don't even read long quotations. Leave them in your brief. Don't risk losing momentum.

Don't memorize your argument. Memorizing your argument word for word may allow you to maintain eye contact and create the illusion of conversation. But as soon as a real conversation starts between you and the judges, your memorized argument will fall as flat as the argument that is read. You can't just walk up to the podium and press "PLAY" in your head. You must have the flexibility to follow wherever the judges lead.

Memorize the substance of your argument, but generally let the wording come spontaneously. There are only a few places where you should memorize what you're going to say word for word. Memorize the wording of your introduction and conclusion so you can start and finish strong. Memorize key phrases and quotations. You may also want to memorize important transitions. But keep the body of your argument loose. Rely on an outline to keep you on track. Rely on your mastery of the facts and the law to fill in the outline.

Speak up. It's hard to persuade someone who can't hear you. Speak loud enough to be heard by the judge farthest away from you. Don't shout. Don't mumble. Don't force the judges to lipread.

You may have to adjust your volume if there's a microphone at the podium. Assume it has been adjusted so you can speak in a normal conversational voice. Stand up straight behind the podium with your mouth in line with the microphone. If you're tall or short, bend the microphone stand toward you when you first get to the podium. If the stand isn't adjustable, don't change your posture to get your mouth closer to the microphone. This will only guarantee you'll be uncomfortable during—and after—your argument. Instead, just speak a little louder.

Speak at a controlled speed. Talk too fast and you're hard to follow. Talk too slow and you sound unnatural. Talking too slow also makes you dull; there's too much time between words when the listener's mind can wander off. Make a conscious effort to find the right speed if you have a tendency toward either extreme. If you're not sure where the golden mean is, try to match your speed to that of the judges.

Speak at a pitch in the lower end of your range. If sexism is the cause of the general perception that low voices have more authority than high voices, then perhaps as women come to occupy more positions of authority this rule will change. However, to the extent this rule is based on our association of high voices with children and low voices with adults, it's here to stay. Especially if you have a high squeaky voice, try to speak at the lower end of your range.

Use vocal dynamics. Don't drone. Speaking in a monotone works like a horse tranquilizer on your audience. Maintain interest and emphasize important points by varying the volume, speed, pitch, and rhythm of your voice. The words you choose are the lyrics of your argument; your voice supplies the melody and the beat.

Avoid ending a sentence with a rising inflection. It turns a statement into a question and makes you sound unsure of what you're saying.

Rhythmic phrases or sentences can create a dramatic effect: "Valdez paid for this contract. The defendant profited from it. This court should enforce it." You can signal your conclusion with a pattern like this and avoid having to explicitly announce you are concluding.

Getting softer and slower is often more effective for emphasis than getting louder and faster. The listener may put up defenses to a loud and fast barrage but open up when you get soft and slow, allowing your message to slip in. You may even want to pause for a moment right before you make an important point. Or pause right after you've made an important point, to allow it to sink in. Just stop. Then move on.

Take out the "uhs." Most people new to public speaking are uncomfortable with silence. So they unconsciously fill the gaps between words with some sound like "uh," "um," or "er." Kicking this distracting habit takes practice. The first step is to find out whether you're doing it. An audiotape or videotape of yourself arguing will reveal the habit if you haven't noticed it before. The tape will also like, you know, like reveal any other, you know, distracting vocal mannerisms you have. Once you become aware of these mannerisms, concentrate on eliminating as many of them as you can when you practice. Improve your signal-to-noise ratio until your argument is pure signal.

By the way, if you get lost while arguing, don't fill the silence with a long "uhhhhhhhhhhh." Keep quiet. Let the judges think you are pausing for emphasis.

Pronounce words correctly.   Poor pronunciation, like poor grammar, makes you sound poorly educated. Make sure you know the correct pronunciation of every word you use in your argument.

This is trickier than it sounds. Experts often disagree about the correct pronunciation of a word. Some words have more than one acceptable pronunciation. Some are pronounced differently in different parts of the country. And sometimes pronouncing a word in the technically correct way can make you sound like a pedant or a snob.

No word better illustrates the dilemmas posed by pronunciation than "err." This word pops up all the time in oral argument, because usually one side is arguing the trial court erred and the other side is arguing the trial court didn't err. The technically correct pronunciation is "ur," but most earth dwellers pronounce it "air." To a judge who's a stickler, however, "air" may sound like a nail being scraped across a blackboard. "Ur," on the other hand, may make you incomprehensible to a down-to-earth judge, or may make you sound like a pompous show-off. If you're like me—and I know I am—you'll err on the safe side by steering clear of the word altogether. Say the trial court "made an error," "was in error," or "committed reversible error."

Use common sense to decide when to abandon correct pronunciation. A tug-of-war with the court over a word can only distract you and the judges from your argument. If the judges pronounce a word differently, switch to their pronunciation or avoid the word.

Generally avoid foreign words. If you use one, use its American pronunciation. You can't expect the judges to be bilingual.

Sometimes you must use a foreign word or phrase because it's a legal term, such as "quasi in rem" or "caveat emptor." Pronunciation of foreign legal terms can vary greatly from one part of the country to another. For example, "voir dire" is "vwar deer" in the North and "vohr dyre" in the South. Use the pronunciation of your legal community.

Here's a list of words commonly used in oral arguments that raise pronunciation problems. I've written their preferred pronunciations with the accented syllable in bold:

accessory:	ak-**sess**-uh-ree
alleged:	uh-**lejd** (only two syllables)
amenable:	uh-**mee**-nuh-bull
ancillary:	**an**-si-lair-ee
appellee:	ap-uh-**lee**
applicable:	**ap**-li-kuh-bull
certiorari:	sur-shee-oh-**rahr**-ee
commission:	kuh-**mi**-shun
capricious:	kuh-**prish**-us
comparable:	**cahm**-pur-uh-bull
controversial:	kahn-truh-**vur**-shull
disparate:	**dis**-pa-rit
extraordinary:	ek-**stror**-di-nair-ee (don't say the word "extra")
forbade:	for-**bad**
formidable:	**for**-mid-uh-bull
genuine:	**jen**-yoo-in
grievous:	**gree**-vus
harassment:	**har**-iss-ment or huh-**ras**-ment
heinous:	**hay**-nis

homicide:	**hahm**-i-syde
hostile:	**hahs**-till
illustrative:	i-**luss**-truh-tiv
influence:	**in**-floo-ents
inherent:	in-**heer**-ent or in-**hair**-ent
irreparable:	i-**rep**-uh-ruh-bull
irrevocable:	i-**rev**-uh-cuh-bull
juror:	**joor**-ur
negotiate:	ne-**go**-shee-ate
often:	**awf**-en (the "t" isn't sounded)
onerous:	**ahn**-ur-us
penalize:	**pee**-nuh-lyze
preferable:	**pref**-uh-ruh-bull
privilege:	**priv**-uh-lij (three syllables)
supposed:	suh-**pozed** (only two syllables)
vehicle:	**vee**-i-kuhl (usually best pronounced "**kar**")

For an entire book on pronunciation problems, see Charles Elster's *There Is No Zoo in Zoology* (New York: Macmillan, 1990).

But knowledge of correct pronunciation isn't enough. To be easily understood, you must articulate your words clearly. When you mumble you sound like you're hiding something; when you enunciate you sound open and honest. Mumbling is also sloppy, like wearing a rumpled suit to court. Clear speaking suggests clear thinking. It's a mark of professionalism.

Most articulation problems are the result of laziness and bad habits rather than physical causes. Don't turn "going to" into "gunna" or "want to" into "wanna." Leave that to rock singers.

If you know you have trouble articulating a certain word, stay away from it. For example, I have trouble saying "inquiry" with the accent on the first syllable. It usually comes out "**in**-kwuh-wee." Luckily I can use its other acceptable pronunciation: "in-**kwyr**-ee." My friend Anne has trouble with "applicable principle." So she says "rule." Look for alternative pronunciations or synonyms for the words that give you trouble.

Don't magnify your mistakes. If you make a small mistake, don't roll your eyes, shake your head, or mutter an expletive under your breath. A small mistake needn't slow you down or fluster you. Keep moving. Don't take time out from your argument to punish yourself. Save that for later.

If you make a big mistake, admit it and correct it: "I'm sorry, Your Honors, I meant to say the trial court found the defendant *not* guilty." Do the same if you discover you've been making the same small mistake over and over: "Your Honors, I apologize. I've been referring to the restaurant as 'One Swell Foop' when in fact it is 'One Fell Swoop.'"

If you lose your train of thought, it will be obvious to the judges. So you might as well admit it and start over: "I'm sorry, Your Honor, I lost my train of thought. What I meant to say was. . . ." Cut your losses.

Adjust your intensity to the distance between you and the judges. Obviously, the greater the distance between you and the judges, the louder you must speak. But you must adjust other aspects of your delivery as well. When the distance is great, your gestures should be large, your facial expressions broad. You also can turn up the intensity of your emotion. Conversely, if you're right on top of the judges, turn everything down. Nobody likes to listen to an oration at the dinner table. A good rule of thumb is: If you're spraying the judges with spit, you're too intense for the distance between you.

6 Substance

Substance is what wins cases. Don't misinterpret the size of this chapter to mean substance is less important than the techniques filling the rest of this book. Not much can be said about substance because it varies with each case. Many techniques, on the other hand, are appropriate to almost every case. But substance is the cargo of your argument; technique is merely the vehicle.

Gear your argument to the standard of review. If you're a first-year law student, the standard of review may seem like an obscure, abstract, legal technicality. But the standard of review determines how hard it will be to get an appellate court to reverse the decision of a trial court or administrative agency. It is often foremost in the minds of appellate judges, and it can mean life or death to an appeal.

The basic dividing line is between the standard of review applied to issues of law and the standard of review applied to issues of fact. On an issue of law, the appellate court is free to substitute its judgment for a trial judge's judgment. This standard is called de novo or plenary review. On an issue of fact, the appellate court is much more constrained. It cannot substitute its judgment on a finding of fact unless a trial judge's finding was clearly erroneous, a jury's finding was unreasonable, or an administrative agency's finding was not supported by substantial evidence. Winning an appeal on an issue of fact is therefore much harder than winning on an issue of law.

But this explanation is true only in general terms. There are other standards of review. Complex issues can arise in determining the applicable standard. And the law in this area

can change. You must research the particular standard of
review applicable to each issue in your case.

Then you must gear your argument on each issue to meet
the standard. When the standard favors you—such as when you
are the appellee and the appellant is challenging a trial court's
finding of fact—it may be your strongest argument. When the
standard goes against you, roll up your sleeves.

Keep it simple. Two aspects of oral argument require you to
make your argument as simple as possible. First, your time is
limited; usually you have no more than twenty minutes. Second,
most people cannot absorb complex information through their
ears.

So don't try to do too much. Don't make every possible
argument; pick your battles. Don't try to cover everything that's
in your brief. Avoid presenting complex legal arguments that
are easier to follow on paper. Pick a few important points that
lend themselves to oral presentation and hammer them home.
If you do a good job, the judges will go back to your brief for
the rest.

**Assume the judges have only a basic familiarity with your case
unless they show you differently.** Another reason to keep your
argument simple is that the judges may not have read the briefs.
Some judges always read them. Others rely on bench memos,
prepared by their clerks or court staff, that summarize the case.
Others may come to an oral argument knowing nothing at all
about the case. You're especially likely to face a judge who
knows nothing about your case in a busy trial court.

An appellate court in which the judges generally read the
briefs before an oral argument is known as a "hot bench." One
in which the judges don't is known as a "cold bench." You may
be able to find out ahead of time which kind of court you're
facing, possibly from the clerk of court. But even if you can,
you can't be sure whether all the judges have read the briefs for
your particular argument. Because you can't be sure, it's better

to err on the side of safety and assume they know little. It's hard to persuade someone who doesn't know what you're talking about. If it becomes clear that the judges are intimately familiar with your case, you can increase the level of complexity of your argument.

Pay close attention to the judges, especially at the beginning of your argument. If you're telling them something they already know, they may give you some indication that they already know it. For example, if you're explaining the facts, and a judge interrupts to ask a question about a legal issue, it's a sign the court already knows the facts and isn't interested in hearing you repeat them. Or a judge may tell you explicitly how much the court knows and what it wants to hear: "Counsel, we're familiar with the facts. Please move on to the constitutional issue." When the court tells you what to do, do it.

Focus on key facts. Although appellate judges are generally supposed to decide legal issues, they often decide who should win a case because of the facts. Then they look (or have a law clerk look) to see whether the law will allow them to do what they believe is fair and just.

But often you can't present the facts from start to finish in an oral argument. First, you don't have time. Second, appellate courts are too busy to get deeply into the facts of each case they must decide, and will use the standard of review to avoid factual issues. Third, if the judges have read the briefs, they often consider it a waste of time to hear you recite the facts. They would rather have you get right to your legal argument. Or they would rather get right to asking you questions about the points troubling them. When the judges don't want to hear the facts, they won't hesitate to cut you off.

If you want to stress the facts of your case, you must overcome these obstacles. Even though the judges may not want to hear much about your facts, oral argument may be your most effective time to present them. Appellate judges are completely cut off from contact with anyone involved in your case. They don't see the witnesses or the parties. At least during oral argument they finally see a flesh-and-blood human being involved in your case: you. If you need to emphasize the flesh and blood of your case to win, this may be your best chance. To increase the likelihood that the judges will listen to your facts, you must make them brief, easy to follow, and interesting.

Make your facts brief by selecting only the key ones. Eliminate references to the record. Leave those in the brief. Eliminate explanations of who testified to what, except when it's critical to an understanding of the importance of a fact. Eliminate unnecessary detail. Cut to the chase.

Make your facts easy to follow by telling a story. Give the facts chronologically from your client's point of view. Avoid complicating the story with unnecessary dates. Instead, explain events in relation to one another whenever possible with phrases like "the following morning" or "two months later." Be sure the story makes sense. Explain why things happened the way they did.

Make your facts interesting with well-chosen details. Turn stick figures into human beings. If you represent the government, a corporation, or some other large organization, personalize your client as much as possible. Find an individual within the organization to focus on. Make your client come alive to the court.

Try to appear objective. Don't leave out critical facts, even if they hurt you. Don't go outside the record. Don't make up facts; fill gaps in the facts only with indisputable inferences. Let the facts speak for themselves. Don't add unnecessary adjectives. Rely instead on selection, arrangement, and emphasis to make them persuasive.

Mix some argument into your facts if you want to. In a brief, your statement of the facts must remain uncontaminated by argument. Oral argument is more flexible. For example, while stating the facts, you might draw the judges' attention to a key fact and mention that it's the linchpin of your argument:

Regan did not know Mehta. He'd never even met him. This makes the jury's finding of malice unreasonable.

But often nothing you can do will keep the judges from telling you to move on to your legal arguments. If you're determined to focus the judges' attention on your facts, your fallback strategy must be to work them into your legal arguments piecemeal. When you do this you must still try to make your facts vivid and compelling while squeezing them into your argument in brief bursts at appropriate times.

Strip the authority you use to the bare essentials. Technical legal arguments work best in writing, where intricate logical relationships can be laid out for the eye to follow. Use only as much authority in your oral argument as you require to lay out the rules governing your case. Leave the details of that authority in your brief. For the average case you rely on, all you'll need to state is the rule or holding. If the case is critical or its applicability is disputed, you'll need to give more. You may need to state the facts of the case or the reasoning behind its rule or holding. State only as much as you have to.

Minimize the clutter of citations. Case citations are best left to the briefs. If a rule is well established, you don't need to refer to any case. Just state the rule. When you do refer to a case, instead of giving a full citation, introduce it with no more than (1) its name or a simplified name, (2) the name of the court that decided it, and (3) the year it was decided or a general description of when it was decided. You can give these in any order:

In the *Chatlos* case, decided by the Third Circuit in 1987, the court held. . . .

In *Chatlos Systems v. National Cash Register Corporation*, decided a few years ago, the Third Circuit held. . . .

A few years ago, the Third Circuit held in *Chatlos* that. . . .

Or you can simply refer the court to your brief:

> In *Chatlos*, cited on page six of our brief, the court held. . . .

> In *Chatlos*, cited in our brief, the court held. . . .

Avoid long citations to statutes and other authority too. Simplify your references to them in any reasonable way.

Add a policy argument if you've got a good one. You won't score any points with a vague argument that something is consistent or inconsistent with "public policy." You must tell the court exactly how a decision in your favor would be good for the real world or the judicial system:

> An employer must be able to speak freely when giving a job reference about a former employee without fear of being sued for defamation. Otherwise, businesses aren't going to be able to adequately screen job applicants and are going to get stuck with dishonest or inferior employees.

> If children can sue their parents for negligence, the courts will be flooded with fraudulent claims by families trying to collect insurance under their homeowners' policies.

Show the court how your case fits into the greater scheme of things.

Policy arguments work best with the highest court in a jurisdiction. Intermediate courts of appeal generally see themselves as error-correcting courts, applying the law as it is. The highest court in a jurisdiction is more free to base its decisions on policy arguments and to change the law when it believes it necessary.

Policy arguments usually work best in conjunction with arguments based on precedent. But sometimes policy is all you've got. There's an old saying that goes "If you're weak on the law, pound the facts. If you're weak on the facts, pound the law. If you're weak on both, pound the table." If you're weak on the facts and the law, argue policy.

Find a theme. Books, plays, movies, and musical works have themes. Arguments should have them too. A theme captures the essence of the case. It ties together the often scattered bits of fact and law out of which your case is constructed. It focuses the judges' attention on what's really important in the new data inundating them. When you find the underlying theme that brings order to surface chaos, you offer the court a key that unlocks your case.

A theme can be a single word that runs through your argument, like "responsibility" in a negligence case, or "promise" in a contract case. Or it might be an underlying policy, like "separation of powers" in a constitutional law case, or "deterrence of police misconduct" in a criminal case. Or it might be a specific aspect of the facts, like the "hypocrisy" of the opposing party or the "daisy chain" in a conspiracy case. Whatever your theme, try to make it memorable. When the judges dump your case out of their short-term memories, you want something to remain.

Pinpoint what was reversible error by the lower court. If you're the appellant, you can't just say the lower court's decision was wrong. You must specify exactly what the lower court did that constituted reversible error. The more precise you are, the better your chances of success.

Rely on the lower court's opinion if it's well reasoned or well written. Although a trial court's opinion has no precedential value on legal issues, one in your favor at least shows that a judge agreed with your position. If the lower court was an intermediate appellate court, your reason for relying on its opinion is much stronger. If any lower court's opinion in your case is well reasoned or well written, milk it for all it's worth. If the lower court agreed with you on a particular argument, mention that when you make the argument. If the lower court eloquently agreed with you, quote its opinion.

Offer the court an easy way to rule in your favor. Judges are like everybody else. They want to avoid difficult decisions. They want to avoid unnecessary conflict and controversy. Accommodate these natural tendencies. Show the judges the easiest way to reach the result you want. Offer them ways to avoid reaching issues they don't have to reach. Don't ask the court to depart from precedent if the facts of an earlier case can be distinguished. Don't ask the court to overturn a statute if you can show the statute doesn't apply. Be explicit: "If the court finds that Smith's conduct did not come within the statute, the court will not have to reach the constitutional issue." Show them a shortcut.

7 Structure

Start strong. First impressions are critical. When the court indicates it's your turn to argue, pick up your outline and whatever else you need and walk confidently to the podium. When you've got everything arranged at the podium, look up at the judges and start talking.

Don't wait until all the judges are looking at you before starting. If two judges are talking to each other, you may want to stall for a couple seconds by pretending to arrange your notes. That way you may be able to avoid interrupting them. But if more than a couple seconds pass and you still don't have the judges' full attention, just barrel into your argument. If you stand there waiting too long, you'll seem either timid—like a kid afraid to ring a doorbell—or passive-aggressive—your silence a reproach to the judges. Command their attention. After the first few words are out of your mouth, you'll get it.

The first words you utter are a salutation to the court determined by tradition. The standard line is "May it please the court." It is acceptable everywhere. "If the court please" and "Your Honors" are acceptable alternatives in some courts.

Next, tell the court your name and who you represent: "My name is Alan Dworsky and I represent the appellant in this case, Linda Chen." The phrase "for the record" is unnecessary. Don't say "I'm *a representative of* the appellant, Linda Chen." This implies you actually work for Chen and are not merely her lawyer.

If rebuttal time is not automatically set aside for appellants or reserved by arrangement with the court clerk, reserve it: "I would like to reserve three minutes for rebuttal." Memorize these formalities. If you're really nervous, write them out in full as a crutch in case your memory fails.

Introduce your argument in a way that is informative, interesting, and persuasive. When you finish the opening formalities, you must orient the court to your case before you can begin your argument. There is much to be accomplished in this introduction. If you're the appellant, in a very few words tell the court:

1. the kind of case it is,
2. the critical facts,
3. the issues you will argue,
4. your position on the issues,
5. the result in the lower court,
6. the standard of review,
7. what you want the court to do.

Try to convey all this information in a persuasive way that grabs the judges' attention. Memorize your entire introduction so you are assured of eye contact during this critical stage of the argument.

If you're the appellee, leave out information that simply repeats what the appellant said, such as the kind of case it is and the result in the lower court. Focus your introduction on the critical facts and your position on the issues.

You don't have to cover each item listed above separately. You can blend more than one together or cover some by implication. You can also vary the order to fit your case. Whatever order you use, don't wait too long to get to the critical facts. They capture the court the quickest. Here's an example of an appellant's introduction that begins with the facts:

> May it please the court. My name is Alan Dworsky and I represent the appellant, Home Finance. I would like to reserve three minutes for rebuttal.
> In this case, by falsifying purchase agreements and credit

histories, the defendants fraudulently induced Home Finance to make more than a million dollars in home loans that later went bad.   They had the help of Home Finance's own president in this scheme.   The defendants paid him $100,000 for conspiring with them.   Because Home Finance's own president knew about the scheme, the trial court granted summary judgment against Home Finance on its fraud claim. The court reasoned that Home Finance hadn't relied on any of the defendants' statements because its own president knew they were false.

The issue before this court is when the knowledge of an officer should be imputed to the corporation. I will show that knowledge is not imputed when the officer is acting adversely to the corporation. This is an issue of law on which this court can freely substitute its judgment for that of the trial court. This court should therefore reverse the granting of summary judgment and remand this case for a full trial on the merits.

If you are arguing several issues, list them. This gives the court a menu it can select from if it's interested in one issue in particular. Tell the court if you're omitting any issues argued in your brief: "I will not be arguing the statutory issue unless the court has questions about it. I will rely on the argument in my brief on that issue." If you've divided your argument with a teammate, tell the court how you've divided it. This will help prevent the judges from questioning you about an issue you're not fully prepared on. But don't stop after stating the issues; always go on to state your position on each one.

When you state your position on an issue, tell the court what you will "show" or "establish": "I will show that knowledge is not imputed when the officer is acting adversely to the corporation." Don't tell the court what you will "attempt to show." This implies you are uncertain whether you will succeed. Don't tell the court what you will "argue." This implies there are two plausible positions on the issue. Also, don't tell the court what you will "prove." "Prove" is what you do on issues of fact at trial, not what you do with issues on appeal.

Finally, don't introduce your argument by saying something like "For the next twenty minutes, I will show. . . ." First, you don't know what you're going to be showing for the next twenty minutes because that may be determined by the judges' questions. This introduction implies you haven't left time for questions and aren't interested in having a conversation. Second, you extinguish any glimmer of hope the judges may have had that you won't use every minute of your allotted time. Your argument should end when it's over. When you give your introduction, the only thing you'll know for sure is that it will all be over within twenty minutes.

After the introduction, move to the facts. If you are the appellant, use your rendition of the facts to get the court on your side. If the court tells you it's familiar with the facts and wants you to move on to your legal argument, move on.

If you are the appellee, after your introduction you should generally move to the facts as the appellant did. You will have listened carefully to the appellant's statement of the facts and noted any important misstatements or omissions. But your statement of the facts should not be limited to simply correcting the appellant's statement. If that's all you do, you will be implicitly accepting the appellant's framework. You will be arguing on the appellant's turf.

Instead, you should reorient the court by using the facts to set up your own framework. Because the court has already heard the facts once from the appellant, your version is going to have to be very compressed. But no matter how brief it is, it should stand on its own. Emphasize essential facts that support your case. Along the way, also point out any important facts the appellant misstated or omitted.

If you are the appellant, after the facts move to your strongest argument. Oral argument is no place for a long, slow build-up. You may get derailed by questions from the judges and never get to your climax. If you do get there, you may have lost the judges' attention along the way. Pick your best shot and start with it.

Some lawyers break this rule for strategic and logical reasons by starting with their argument for complete relief even if it's weaker than their argument for partial relief. For example, if they are requesting a complete reversal under one argument and a new trial under another, they put their argument for reversal first even if it's weaker. That way they avoid the backward logic of saying "I want a piece of cake, but if you won't give it to me, I want the whole cake." Other lawyers would rather go forward using backward logic than put a weak argument first.

If you are the appellee, you must be flexible in choosing which argument to start with. Your plan as appellee going into the argument should be to start with your strongest argument for upholding the decision of the lower court. But you must remain open to changing that plan in response to how the appellant's argument goes. An appellant with more than one argument for reversal only needs to win one of them. You have to win them all to preserve the victory you won in the lower court.

Listen carefully to the judges' questions to the appellant for clues about where you're vulnerable. If you can tell you're in deep trouble on an issue, make that issue your first priority. Start there, even if it's your weakest argument, and give it all you've got. What you thought was your strongest issue will be irrelevant if you don't win your weakest one.

Adjust your argument to other things you notice during the appellant's argument. If the court shows it agrees with your position on an issue, don't waste time discussing it. If the court shows a particular interest in an issue or some particular concern about it, discuss it fully.

Reviving a question a judge asked the appellant can provide a smooth and effective transition into your argument. This is especially true if the appellant's answer to the question was weak. This strategy also has the advantage of beginning your conversation with the judges immediately. The earlier you establish a connection with the court, the stronger your relationship will be.

You don't have to follow the order set by the appellant in making your arguments. Although that structure makes your argument easy to follow, it is often poor strategy because it implies—at least in part—that you accept the appellant's view of the case. As much as possible, choose a structure that reflects your view of the case. Weave your counterarguments into that structure.

Give the court signposts. Signposts are even more important in speech than in writing. In a brief, readers can look back to get their bearings if they are lost. In an oral argument, listeners are totally dependent on the speaker's voice for orientation. You should therefore use more transitions in oral argument than you do in a brief.

The most effective transitions point both ways. They refer back to what you have just said and point forward to what you are about to say. Logically, they should do both in order. Suppose you've just finished arguing that a statute violates the due process clause and are about to argue that it violates the equal protection clause. Your transition should go something like this: "Not only does the statute violate the due process clause, but it violates the equal protection clause as well." And you're off and running about equal protection. It's that simple.

Because a listener is totally dependent on you for orientation, your signposts can repeat points without seeming redundant. Your transition may sum up all your main preceding points before leading to the next point: "I've shown A, B, and C, and now I will show D."

Integrate your signposts into your argument. They shouldn't seem like you just stuck them in; they should sound natural.

Leave time for your conclusion. You can't finish strong if you don't get to your conclusion or if you run out of time in the middle of it.   Plan to complete your argument with time to spare. Finishing before time is called shows you are in control of your argument and inspires confidence.

Don't feel you have to fill every second you're allowed. Use only as much time as you need. If you finish five minutes early, fine. Sit down. The judges will appreciate your brevity. And they will resent you if you pad your argument just to fill the time.

Running out of time is unavoidable and excusable only when the judges have kept you from your conclusion with their questions.   If your time runs out while you're answering a question, you can finish your answer and then ask the court's permission for extra time: "I see my time has run out.   May I have an extra minute to conclude?"   If the judges know their questions have prevented you from reaching your conclusion, they will usually grant your request. Just don't be rude by taking more than the extra minute you requested.

Finish strong.   Final impressions are as important as first impressions. Memorize your conclusion, just as you memorized your introduction.   Finishing with good eye contact is critical.

Start your conclusion by letting the judges know it's coming. When they hear "In conclusion" their attention level shoots up. They know they're almost to the finish line and they expect to hear something important.   Letting them know your conclusion is coming also gives them a last chance to ask questions. You can even invite final questions by saying "If there are no further questions" and then pausing for a moment while making eye contact.   If no questions come, then follow through with your conclusion.

You don't necessarily have to signal your conclusion by saying "In conclusion" or words to that effect.   You can signal it indirectly by briefly summarizing your main points.   Another way is to make your language more dramatic.   Plain English should be the main dish of your argument, but if you like you can serve a rich dessert at the end.   Or you can use a series of parallel or rhythmic sentences. If you have a knack for beautiful rhetoric, the place for it is in your conclusion.

The last thing you say should be a simple statement of what you want the court to do. If you're the appellee, this will generally be some variation of "We therefore ask that this court affirm the judgment of the trial court." If you're the appellant there are more possibilities, but the format is the same: "We therefore ask that this court reverse the judgment of the trial court on liability and remand this case for a new trial on damages." Don't say "please," as in "We ask this court to please reverse the judgment of the trial court." It sounds like you're begging.

Don't dribble off. Don't gather up your outline and other papers while you're finishing. Follow through with good delivery to the very end. After you've told the court what you want it to do, pause and maintain eye contact with the judges for a second. This will give the judges one last chance to ask a question. If you don't get a question in that second, say "Thank you." Wait another second to allow the judges to say "Thank you, counsel." Then pick up your outline and other papers and walk confidently back to your seat.

8 Questions

Questions are gifts. Don't be afraid of questions from the judges. Welcome them. They allow you to truly know your audience. They show what's on the judges' minds so you can tailor your argument accordingly. They reveal judges' misunderstandings that you otherwise would never have known about or had a chance to correct. They show that the court is interested in your argument. They transform your argument into a conversation. Rejoice when you get that first question from the bench. You're not alone on the dance floor anymore; a judge has asked you to dance.

Most questions are motivated by a judge's desire to simply understand your argument. Sometimes a question is an attack on your argument, but what sounds like an attack may be motivated by a judge's desire to help you. The judge may agree with your position and be using you to persuade the other judges. Or the judge may simply be testing your argument to remove a few remaining doubts that stand in the way of a decision in your favor. So avoid treating a question as an attack. Don't take it personally. Even if it's clearly hostile, don't be hostile back. Explain, don't retaliate.

Stop talking when a judge asks a question and keep quiet until the judge finishes. Judges are allowed to be rude. When a judge asks you a question, stop talking immediately. Stop even if the judge is interrupting you in the middle of a sentence or interrupting your answer to a previous question. Don't resent the judge's rudeness. It's efficient. It saves you precious seconds. Imagine that the interrupting judge is saying: "I'm sorry to interrupt, counsel, but although what you're saying is very interesting, there are more pressing matters we'd like to get to before your time runs out."

You, on the other hand, must have better manners. Never interrupt a judge. Never. This is easy to forget in the heat of an argument. But oral argument isn't like some TV game show where contestants score points by answering a question before the moderator has finished asking it. Wait patiently until a judge finishes asking a question before you answer it.

Listen carefully to questions. Don't stop listening as soon as you hear a few key words in a judge's question and start composing the answer in your mind. Listen carefully all the way to the end. You need to know the exact question the judge is asking so you can answer it properly.

To show you're listening, maintain eye contact with the judge asking the question. Don't use the question as an opportunity to check your outline or the clock. If a judge asks a stupid question, don't roll your eyes or let your jaw drop. Keep a straight face.

Ask for clarification if you don't understand a question. Don't answer a question you don't understand. It's a gamble you can't afford to lose. There are lots of ways to ask for clarification. If you haven't got a clue, you can simply say: "I'm sorry, Your Honor, but I didn't understand the question." If you think you're close, you can paraphrase: "Are you asking whether the police had probable cause?" You can even ask for a little help: "Was that the case where the police stopped the suspect based on a drug dealer profile?"

Your words and tone of voice should convey that neither you nor the judge is at fault for your confusion. They should convey that your inability to understand the question has resulted neither from the judge's failure to ask it clearly nor from your lack of intelligence or preparation. They should convey simply that you consider the question important and want to make sure you understand it.

Asking for clarification is an exception to the rule that you can't ask the judges questions. Other exceptions include questions related to procedural matters, such as whether you can submit a supplemental memorandum or take a minute to conclude after questions have used up your time. But you shouldn't ask a question related to the substance of your argument, such as "Don't you think, Your Honor, that a tenant should be free from this kind of harassment from a landlord?" This is a breach of protocol that may make the judges uncomfortable or even angry. You can't have a normal human conversation with the judges. At best, oral argument is a peculiar form of conversation in which one side gets to ask all the important questions.

Think before you answer. There's no shame in pausing before answering a question. In fact, if you answer too quickly, it may look like you haven't considered the question fully. By taking a moment to think before answering, you show respect for the depth of the question asked and indirectly for the judge who asked it. Pausing to think when you need to also helps prevent you from giving a stupid answer.

Of course, even pausing doesn't guarantee a perfect answer. The perfect answer usually comes while you're driving home after the argument. Don't kick yourself because you didn't think of it at the podium. Don't replay the argument over and over in your head, dwelling on what you should have said. You did the best you could at the time. Remember all the things you did right. Find the lesson in any mistake you made. Then let go and move on.

Never put off answering a question until later in the argument. Never say: "I will be getting to that in just a few minutes, Your Honor, under my second point." You will appear evasive. You will irritate the judge who asked the question. You will miss the chance to answer the question when it's fresh, before it goes stale in the judge's mind. You may even run out of time before you get to the answer or simply forget to answer the question later. Avoid these pitfalls. Answer a question when it's asked.

Give a direct answer first, then explain. The first word out of your mouth after a judge asks a question should be "yes" or "no" or their equivalents, like "certainly" or "absolutely not." If you must hedge, announce it immediately with a word like "possibly." Your direct answer will illuminate any explanation that follows.

Don't take a long path through the forest of your reasoning to get to an answer. The judges may lose interest along the way. They've asked a question; they want an answer. Now. Don't keep them waiting. By giving a direct answer immediately, you satisfy their hunger for the bottom line.

You also avoid appearing evasive even for a moment. Postponement breeds distrust. Directness suggests honesty and confidence. Don't beat around the bush.

If you get a compound question from a judge, you may need to add a brief introduction to your response: "Your Honor, there really are two parts to your question. I'll address the common law issue first and then the statutory issue." You may also need to add an introduction if you get questions from two different judges at once.   Immediately acknowledge the questions of both judges: "I see there are two questions on this issue.   I'll address the common law issue first and then the statutory issue."

Don't introduce an answer by saying you were just about to get to it: "Your Honor, that was my very next point" or "I was just coming to that, Your Honor." This waste words and makes you look infantile.   You don't score points for saying you thought of something first. The judges may even interpret such a statement as criticism, as if you were complaining that they interrupted you.

Don't introduce an answer by flattering the judge who asked it: "That's an excellent question, Your Honor." This also wastes words and makes you sound presumptuous and patronizing.

Your approval implies the power to disapprove. Just answer the question.

Don't explain too much or too little. Avoid the overenthusiasm of the expert initiating the uninformed. My friend Ward is a mechanical wizard. I used to call him whenever anything at my house broke down. But when I asked him how to get my refrigerator running, he'd give me an hour lecture on the physics of refrigeration. I don't call him anymore. If you give the judges more information than they want, they won't call you anymore either.

The judges also won't call if you give them too little information. When I stopped calling Ward, I started calling my friend Jim, who's also a mechanical wizard. But Jim would tell me to "adjust the framistam." I don't know what a framistam is. I need someone to tell me to turn the round thing a half-turn to the right. Remember that the judges probably won't know nearly as much about your case as you do. Don't toss out case names or statute numbers and expect the judges to know what you're talking about. Tell them to turn the round thing a half-turn to the right.

Disagree with judges gracefully. Stand up to the judges when you must to defend your position. When a judge attacks your argument, show respect, but remain steadfast. Remember, the judge is not attacking you personally. Don't get angry, get firm.

Avoid drawing attention to the fact that you are disagreeing with a judge. If you begin a response with that *L.A. Law* phrase "With all due respect, Your Honor," alarms will go off in the judge's mind. And don't say "Your Honor, I wish to respectfully disagree." The judge's mind will skip right over the "respectfully" and land on the "disagree." A situation providing an opportunity for explanation will be transformed into a confrontation.

Be an Aikido master. If you are attacked, gracefully spin and brush the blow past you without injuring your attacker. Do not meet force with force. Turn even a vicious attack into a simple misunderstanding. Don't fight, explain. If you don't tell the judges they're wrong, they won't have to admit it when they discover it. This allows them to save face and makes it easier for them to change their minds.

Don't let hypothetical questions push you into defending an untenable position. Push your arguments as far as the facts and the law will allow, and not one step further. Defending an untenable position will damage your credibility on your tenable positions. Make concessions where you must. When the facts in a hypothetical warrant a different result, concede that. Disarm the court with your frankness and candor. Then, by distinguishing the facts in your case from those in the hypothetical, go on to show how your concessions don't hurt you.

Never concede more than necessary. Anticipate hypothetical questions. Decide ahead of time exactly where your facts would have to be different to warrant a different result. If you try to decide in the heat of your argument, you may paint yourself into a corner.

Never bluff. Honesty is the best policy. If you're stumped by a question, admit it. Say: "I don't know" or "I'm not familiar with that case." If you bluff and get caught, your credibility— the foundation of your entire argument—will be irreparably damaged. Although you may not be finished arguing, your argument will effectively be over. Expect no more questions. The judges won't do anything to prolong your presence before them.

Judges usually draw their questions from what's in the briefs. But even when you've done a thorough job researching, it's possible a judge will ask a question based on authority unfamiliar to you. Sometimes this happens because the judge is approaching the case from a different angle. Sometimes it happens because authority has come out since you updated your research.

When you get a question about authority unfamiliar to you, there are a couple things you can do. You can ask the judge for information about the authority: "Your Honor, I wasn't aware of that case, but if you will summarize it for me I can respond to your question." Or you can ask to submit a supplemental memorandum: "Your Honor, I wasn't aware of that case. If the court will allow, I'd like a chance to review it and submit a memorandum responding to your question." If the court declines your offer, you're out of luck. All you can do then is hope the question wasn't important.

Flow back into your argument after answering a question. After fully answering a question, don't stand there waiting for another question or a response from the judges. Don't ask: "Does that answer your question, Your Honor?" or "May I continue?" Don't imply you were rudely interrupted by saying "Now if I may resume where I left off." Just flow back into your argument. If the transition is really smooth, the court won't be able to tell where your answer to the question ended and the resumption of your argument began.

But don't use this technique in every situation. Watch the judges for nonverbal signs. If you sense they may want to know more, or if you've been answering a series of questions, pause for an instant after your answer to allow another question. You don't want to create the impression you're trying to evade further questions on an issue. Just don't let that brief pause become an awkward silence. If a judge doesn't ask another question immediately, resume your argument.

However you resume your argument, you must decide where to resume it. Sometimes a judge's question indicates the court considers an issue other than the one you were arguing to be more important. When that happens, first answer the particular question. Then present anything else you planned to say on that issue. Seize the moment. Talk about what the judges want to talk about when they want to talk about it. Then go back and cover whatever you skipped in your argument.

Sometimes, however, you must make the difficult choice to talk about what you want to talk about rather than what a judge is interested in. If you have seven judges to persuade, and one of them doesn't understand your argument or wants to talk about some peripheral matter, you shouldn't waste your whole argument on that judge. Go for the majority.

Resisting the majority is the most difficult and risky choice of all. But if it's your only hope for victory, you must attempt it. Answer directly and briefly the questions the judges ask and then steer them back to the issues you believe are decisive. Take control of the wheel when you must. Stay your course.

9 Rebuttal

Always reserve rebuttal time. Some courts don't allow rebuttal, but most do. Of those that do, some automatically allocate a certain amount of time for it. For example, the appellant may be given fifteen minutes for the main argument and five minutes for rebuttal.

In the rest of the courts that allow rebuttal, each appellant is given a certain total amount of time to argue and is allowed to allocate it between the main argument and rebuttal. When you're allowed to do this, allocate almost all your time to your main argument. Reserve only about three minutes for rebuttal.

In some courts you reserve rebuttal by arrangement with the clerk before the argument starts. Otherwise, tell the court at the start of your argument how much time you want to reserve for rebuttal: "May it please the court. My name is Alan Dworsky and I represent Linda Chen. I would like to reserve three minutes for rebuttal." Remember, the time you reserve for rebuttal will be subtracted from the time permitted for your main argument.

Always reserve rebuttal time if you're allowed to. Even if you don't use it, the possibility that you might will make the appellee less likely to misrepresent the facts or the law. And you don't have the option of waiving rebuttal if you haven't reserved it in the first place.

Make all your important points in your main argument. Rebuttal is only a chance for an appellant to briefly refute the appellee's arguments. Raising new issues is improper. If you try to raise a new issue, the judges will probably cut you off.

Go for broke on the issues you argue in your main

argument. Don't hold back anything important in the hope that you can ambush your opponent in rebuttal. If the judges don't hear the point in your main argument, they will assume it wasn't that important. You may not even get a rebuttal if questions from the judges force you to use up your rebuttal time in your main argument. If you do get a rebuttal, you may have other more important things to say and not enough time. Or the judges may have made up their minds before you get to your rebuttal. Or they may simply be tired. No matter how delicious it is, if you save that special dish for the end of the meal, the judges may be too full to take a bite.

Listen carefully to your opponent's argument. If you are the appellant, naturally you'll be relieved when you're done with your main argument. You've survived. But it's not over yet. It's too early to relax and daydream. You must be as alert during the appellee's argument as you were during your own. Listen carefully to every word your opponent says. Take note of any serious misrepresentation of fact or law. Also listen to the judges carefully. Take note of any indication from them that an argument made by your opponent has scored some points.

If you are an appellee, your main argument should include your rebuttal of the appellant's argument. Using the briefs, determine ahead of time the best way to weave a rebuttal into your argument. But having a prepared rebuttal doesn't mean you can rehearse your argument in your head one last time while the appellant is arguing. You must focus completely on the appellant's argument and the judges' questions. Adjust your argument to rebut any unexpected points made by the appellant and to address any unexpected concerns displayed by the judges.

Don't waste time on an introduction. You don't have time for an introduction in your rebuttal. The most you have time for is a single line telling the court how many points you intend to cover: "Your Honors, I have only two brief points on rebuttal. First, . . ." You can use a line like this to reassure the judges that you're not going to say much. Practice truth in advertising; don't announce you have two points and then make three.

Another way to start is to simply dive right into your first point: "Contrary to what the Government said, the defendant was not identified in a line-up but rather in a one-person show-up." In rebuttal, you don't have to start with "May it please the court" or any other traditional phrase as you do at the start of your main argument.

Don't forget that the judges may ask questions during rebuttal. A single question can easily eat up your time. So when you start your rebuttal, you'd better get your points out in a hurry.

Clearly connect each point you make to a point you're trying to refute. Your strategy as an appellant in rebuttal is different from your strategy in your main argument. Your main argument is often stronger if you present it without making reference to the appellee's arguments. Spend your time there selling your product, not disparaging your competitor's.

Rebuttal, on the other hand, should be used to directly attack specific points or arguments made by the appellee. Don't rely on the court to connect your points on rebuttal to arguments made by the appellee. Show the court the connection: "*Chatlos*—relied on heavily by IBM—is distinguishable from our case. It involved a commercial buyer, not a consumer. Consumer claims like the one in our case are judged according to a more lenient standard under the UCC."

If you must repeat something from your main argument, say it in a new way. Rebuttal is not a chance to have the last word by merely repeating an argument you've already made. If something you said in your main argument clearly refutes the appellee's argument, don't repeat it on rebuttal.

Sometimes, however, you know that what you said refutes a particular point made by the appellee, but you're not confident that it's clear to the judges. To play it safe in this situation, you should explicitly make the connection for the judges, even if it means repeating yourself.

The key is to repeat yourself without appearing to do so. Make your argument sound new by emphasizing the connection between it and one of the appellee's arguments. Or customize your earlier argument to refute a particular point. Avoid introducing a point on rebuttal with phrases like "As I said in my main argument" or "As I pointed out earlier." Also avoid "re" words such as "repeat," "reiterate," "restate," or "re-emphasize."

Don't try to rebut everything your opponent says. Comment only on serious misrepresentations of fact or law and arguments that seriously hurt your position. Resist the temptation to nitpick. It makes you look desperate. And the clutter of little points may obscure your main points. Keep your eye on the big picture. For the same reasons you picked a few good arguments to include in your main argument, pick a few good points to make on rebuttal.

If the judges have already corrected a misstatement made by your opponent, don't simply point out the misstatement again. If that's all you do, you'll look like you're trying to take credit for the judges' discovery. And judges can be insulted when you tell them what they obviously already know. If you're going to bring up a misstatement the judges have already discovered, show how it affects the case. Say something new.

Don't use strong words like "false," "wrong," "incorrect," "misrepresentation," or "misstatement" in referring to your opponent's argument unless the error is objectively verifiable. Misstatements of facts in the record or relevant rules fall in this category. Never use the word "lie" unless you have indisputable evidence that your opponent has made an intentional misstatement.

You should correct a serious misstatement of fact or law even if the misstatement helps you. In addition to fulfilling your ethical obligations to the court, you will increase your credibility

and decrease your opponent's. Chances are the court eventually
will find the error anyway. You have little to lose and much to
gain by pointing it out yourself.

Capitalize on unexpected concessions. If there's a concession
in your opponent's brief, you should capitalize on it in your main
argument.   But there's always a chance your opponent will
concede something new in the oral argument, especially in
response to a question from the court. If you hear a new
concession, pounce on it when it's your turn. Show how it
makes your argument even stronger.

Close quickly. Finishing strong is as important in your rebuttal
as it is in your main argument. Often the strongest way to finish
is to simply complete your final point, say "thank you," and sit
down. You can briefly repeat what you want the court to do if
you need to, such as when your rebuttal relates to some
particular aspect of your requested relief. But don't add the
request for relief as mere boilerplate. In these final moments
before the judges, every word you utter should be meaningful.

Waive your rebuttal time if you don't need it. Use your
rebuttal time only if you think the appellee did some damage to
your position that needs repair. Don't get sucked into an
infantile game of: "Did not." "Did so." "Did not." "Did so."
When the appellee has not scored any points, there's no need
to have the last word.   In fact, there is a considerable
psychological advantage to saying "I waive my rebuttal, Your
Honors." By waiving your rebuttal you are saying "My main
argument was bulletproof. Nothing my opponent said seriously
challenged my argument, so there's no need for me to respond."
This display of confidence and strength may make a stronger
final impression than anything you could say in three minutes.

10 Conclusion

You're ready. You're nervous, but you know how to channel that nervous energy into your performance. You know the facts and the law. You've got your outline. You know the right speaking style. You know how to handle questions. You know the territory of your argument blindfolded, so you can comfortably go in any direction the judges want to. Your clothes are pressed and your shoes are shined. It's time to get excited.

If you're a law student, your first oral argument is going to be the most exciting experience of your law school career. For the first time, you're going to get to look and act like a real lawyer. And for the first time, you're going to feel like a real lawyer. It's a wonderful experience to have in the springtime of your first year of life in the law, when everything is still fresh and new.

But even if this oral argument isn't your first, it's still going to be exciting. Oral argument is intense every time you do it. The thrill never wears off. While you're arguing, the rest of the world doesn't exist. You are drawn into total involvement in the moment, total immersion in the here and now, total aliveness. Oral argument demands all your powers of concentration, thought, and expression. It can be an exhilarating experience of self-actualization. Focus on that possibility. Reach for it.

Then take the rest of the day off.